Reba

It is the courage to
continue that counts.

You can do this.

Emr.

Sir Ranulph Fiennes was the first person to reach both poles by surface travel and the first, with Dr Mike Stroud, to cross the Antarctic continent unsupported. In the 1960s he was removed from the SAS Regiment for misuse of explosives but, after joining the army of the Sultan of Oman, received that country's Bravery Medal on active service in 1971. He was the first person ever to be awarded two clasps to the Polar medal for both the Antarctic and Arctic regions. Fiennes has led over thirty expeditions, including the first polar circum-navigation of the Earth, and in 2003 he ran seven marathons in seven days on seven continents in aid of the British Heart Foundation. In 1993 Her Majesty the Queen awarded Fiennes the Order of the British Empire (OBE) because, on the way to breaking records, he has raised over £18 million for charity. He was named Best Sportsman in the 2007 ITV Great Briton Awards and in 2009 he became the first old-age pensioner to reach the summit of Everest.

Also by Ranulph Fiennes

A Talent for Trouble

Ice Fall in Norway

The Headless Valley

Where Soldiers Fear to Tread

Hell on Ice

To the Ends of the Earth

Bothie the Polar Dog (with Virginia Fiennes)

Living Dangerously

The Feather Men

Atlantis of the Sands

Mind Over Matter

The Sett

Fit for Life

Beyond the Limits

The Secret Hunters

Captain Scott

Mad, Bad and Dangerous to Know

Mad Dogs and Englishmen

Killer Elite

My Heroes

Cold

Agincourt

Heat

Fear: Our Ultimate Challenge

The Elite: the Story of Special Forces

Shackleton: A Biography

Ranulph Fiennes

climb your mountain

*Everyday lessons
from an extraordinary life*

QUERCUS

For Kenton Cool and Ian Parnell;
the Vertigo Removers

CONTENTS

▲

PROLOGUE

▲

THE NIGHTMARE TREK

▲

What is any life but a series of opportunities to grasp and challenges to overcome?

_____

The heaviest sledge-load known to have been pulled by a dog for up to 300 miles weighed 150 pounds – about the same weight as the average man in the street. In 1903, the famous explorers Scott and Shackleton towed loads of 175 pounds each, and on his last, fatal expedition to the South Pole, Scott towed 200 pounds. Reinhold Messner, the world's greatest mountain climber, wrote of a sledge he hauled in Antarctica: 'Two hundred and sixty-four pounds is a load for a horse, not a human being.'

Despite our best efforts to keep to only vital equipment – toothpaste or soap, for instance, were not taken since their absence would not threaten our survival for three months – each of *our* sledges weighed 485 pounds, by far the heaviest one-man sledge-load of any recorded expedition. If you've ever tried to tow a Morris Minor for a short distance, that's what it's like, though imagine doing it ten hours a day for weeks on end. To top it off, we would not just be contending with the sheer difficulty of shifting the sledges; as worrying was the very real danger of taking such a heavy load across thin snow bridges over crevasses.

Ahead of me and my companion, Dr Mike Stroud, lay 1,700 miles, as we strived to become the first people in history to cross the whole Antarctic land mass on foot, without outside support.

We braced ourselves against our dog harnesses and found, to our immense relief, that we could just drag the sledges forward, provided we applied maximum effort at every step. Any obstacle such as a jagged rut of ice was enough to jam the front end of the runners, but it could be done.

We spent twenty-six days merely ascending the Filchner Ice Shelf before we even reached the edge of the actual land mass of Antarctica, the true starting line of any attempt to cross the continent. The ice-shelf was really only a mass of ice grounded on the sea-floor and temporarily attached to the continent. The constant seaward movement of its surface caused a highly lethal crevasse environment. We fell into more than seventy of them over the course of our journey, but the safety ropes between us and our sledges saved us from death, and we were always there to pull each other out.

The sledge harnesses bit into our skin, muscle and tendons. So did our boots. Blisters began to form. The sun and wind started to crack our lips, despite preventative creams. I knew the pattern well. First my inner anger would be directed at the weather, the equipment and the ice. Later, at my companion. The same process would hold good for Mike.

On the first day we stopped, utterly exhausted, after five hours. We had managed four miles. Now we only had another 1,696 miles to go and, since we had food for one hundred days, we would quickly need to find a way of increasing our daily average to sixteen miles. If we did not do so, this daily average would itself shoot up. We could not afford a single rest day, no matter our health or the weather.

Our hands and feet began to blister and became poisoned. We took antibiotics, but there was a limited supply. The skins on our skis loosened and needed constant adjustment with cold, cracked fingers. Our eyes hurt and we sometimes needed to take off our goggles when they froze up. Mike had to keep his off one day in white-out conditions and, that night, suffered the agony of sun-blindness. Amethocaine drops eventually sorted him out.

Throughout the three-month journey, we both remained fearful of crevasses. As with anti-personnel mines in a war

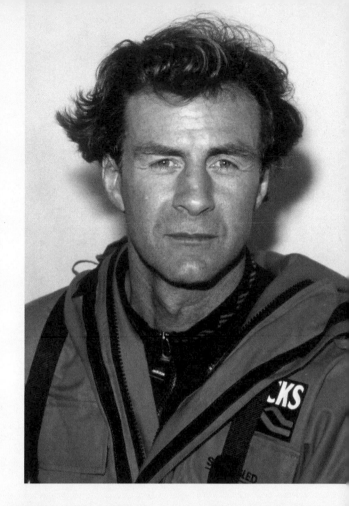

Right: A week before leaving for Antarctica, and several stone heavier than I would finish the expedition.

Below: A load for a horse, not a human being.

Setting out. Note the shine of a crevasse on the horizon ahead.

Above: Dr Mike Stroud contemplates the crevasse from which he was lucky to escape alive.

Left: A collapsed crevasse on the Beardmore glacier.

zone, you only know they are there when you have trodden on one, by which time the information is rather on the late side. The best policy, I discovered, over many expeditions through crevasse fields, was simply to watch the bloke ahead carefully at all times.

Mike's diary entries included: 'Gaping holes left and right, a few yards away in the gloom . . . nerve-racking . . . the bridges are soft and difficult.'

On one occasion, in a thick mist, Mike fell twenty feet into a crevasse, landing on a ledge above a drop with no visible bottom. His heavy sledge, an aerial torpedo, thankfully missed him but struck the crevasse wall and shattered in two. We were blessed with good fortune since the vital runners were not damaged, so repairs were easy.

Our two petrol cookers suffered from leakage problems around the washers and caused a number of fires in the tent during the journey. We repaired much broken gear using our penknives, tweezers, and metal cut from empty fuel bottles.

We progressed to nine-hour travel days, but still averaged only ten miles. We needed to get rid of weight now in time to make enough mileage to keep the target feasible. The time to take hard decisions was quickly upon us, and we took the difficult decision to bury our extra warm clothes. We knew they would be vital as we climbed higher and temperatures plummeted. Maybe we would have second thoughts later. But there would be no 'later' if we could not get a move on now. So just like the soap and the toothpaste, the clothes were sacrificed.

As we continued hauling through a disturbed zone of the Filchner, an extraordinary phenomenon occurred. The ice-shelf entered a hyperactive phase for no apparent reason, causing hitherto 'safe' snow bridges to collapse into the great crevasses that laced the entire feature. And we were caught in the middle. Each sudden implosion was accompanied by a thunderous roar and clouds of snow vapour rising high in the air as if from a geyser. One gaping hole, which opened up a mere ten paces ahead of Mike, was 45 feet wide by 120 feet in length, and lay directly across our intended route.

All around us new explosions announced further craters. We must escape to a safer area. But where was safer? At any moment we expected to be plunged into an abyss. We headed towards the distant hump of Berkner Island as fast as we could move. Time stood still. For an hour our luck held. But then one immense crater appeared immediately between us, and for a moment there was solid ice ahead of me, and in the next moment Mike's ski-trail had vanished. The roar of imploding snow dropping into the bowels of the ice-shelf boomed up in successive echoing waves from the blue pit, into which dropped the safety rope that joined us. Late that night we reached Berkner and camped on solid ice with a luxurious feeling of safety.

'To avoid being crushed by the very thought of what lay ahead, I forced myself to concentrate only on a much closer goal.'

As our physical condition deteriorated, the enormity of our task, the discomfort to be lived with, minute by minute, hour by hour and yard by yard, sank in, so that it became increasingly unthinkable that we could tolerate this burden for another hundred, never mind over 1,600, miles. To avoid being crushed by the very thought of what lay ahead, I forced

---

myself to concentrate only on a much closer goal, such as the camp that night, or merely the next sixty minutes, when I could eat a rationed chocolate square.

With self-imposed blinkers to enable this 'sectioning of the whole' method, I was just able to cope mentally with the appalling distances and physical hardship.

As with many a previous polar journey, including those of Scott and Shackleton, Mike and I suffered from a competitive hostility. Which of us pulled better and faster? Who was pulling too hard and risking hypothermia? Who was not pulling hard enough and thus lessening our chances of success? All this became a constant mental refrain.

From a practical point of view, I used my competitive hostility towards Mike to help me in my ongoing internal fight against the wimpish voice forever telling me to give up due to exhaustion, bodily pains and the increasingly cold temperatures. 'Yes, I want to stop,' I muttered back to this voice, 'but not before Mike does.' This was a wonderful incentive to continue. I used my churning thoughts of hostility as something to concentrate on, an occupational therapy to keep my mind off self-pity. I have always liked being in a team, but it is darkly curious to reflect now, looking back, that the most difficult expeditions of all are solo, not because you have no one to share the experience with, but because you have nobody to hate.

▲

As we pushed hard and climbed into the rarefied polar air at 10,000 feet, Mike's experimental notes recorded: 'Ran was at times using nearly 10,000 calories a day. This is more than has been documented ever for any length of time.'

We were losing muscle and weight from our hearts as well as our body mass. On Day 51, Mike weighed us in the tent.

'Ran,' he recorded, 'has lost 40 pounds and me 30 pounds. Twenty per cent of our body weights.'

Two days later Mike developed terrible diarrhoea and said we must stop. Instead of being sympathetic I was furious. After two hours in the tent and drinking hot tea, he forced himself into his harness. But three hours later he collapsed in the snow. I regretted my lack of sympathy immediately. It caused the one bad blip in the many journeys we have done together before and since. It was a mistake I never repeated.

Close to the Pole our progress was pitiful, but we lengthened our hours and tramped on. Mike told me: 'If things go on like this beyond the Pole, I can see myself wanting out. I simply don't have the same resolve as you.' He wrote, 'Nausea and abdominal pains through the first hour. The whole day was long and hellish.'

About twelve miles short of the Pole, Mike spent a few seconds too long doing up his trouser fly with his mitts off at minus 90° wind chill. He tried to force his already numb fingers back into his mitts, but could not. He cried out with pain. I took my mitts off to try to help him, but my own fingers quickly lost feeling and were useless. He managed just in time to force his hands down his trousers into his crotch. His fingers were badly nipped and blistered, but not permanently damaged.

A few hours later he became hypothermic. He knelt and stared vacantly into space, ignoring the intense cold.

I pitched the tent and, after hot soup and an hour's sleep, Mike began to focus again. His memory, which had entirely gone as far as the last few hours were concerned, slowly returned.

Later that day Mike said that he would try to go on. His resilience was remarkable. At 7 p.m. on our sixty-eighth day of travel, we arrived at the South Pole. We had man-hauled

The author and Dr Mike Stroud spend barely an hour at the
South Pole before pushing on.

700 miles and felt as though we had come to the end of our tether.

Our Norwegian rival Kagge had altered his original plan to cross Antarctica to an attempt to reach the Pole solo and unsupported. Our problem was that of putting Norwegians on a pedestal and feeling inferior. The danger of such an illusion is a loss of self-belief, of the confidence necessary to keep battling on. But there is also, of course, the danger of blindly determining to keep going at all costs instead of recognising the need to turn back – to fail, but to live to fight another day.

Scott made the South Pole but died on his way back to base, having exhausted his supplies, whereas Shackleton, a few years before, turned back just before reaching the Pole and, as a result, just made it back alive to his ship. His policy was 'better a live donkey than a dead lion'.

Wise advice.

We spent one hour in our tent at the Pole and then continued.

▲

I have lived a long, full life and been fortunate in surviving a great number of expeditions to the ends of the Earth, to the edge of what was once thought physically possible. A natural question anyone might ask is: *why?* Why attempt such challenges, at the absolute limits of what the human body can stand? Why push on, when the more sensible course would be to stop, and to live a quieter life, a more ordinary life?

The great mountaineer George Mallory wrote: 'If one should ask me what "use" there was in climbing, or attempting to climb the world's highest peak, I would be compelled to answer, "None." There is no scientific end to be served; simply the gratification of the impulse of achievement, the indomitable desire to see what lies beyond that ever beats within the heart of man.'

When boiled down, however, what is any life but a series of opportunities to grasp and challenges to overcome? You may not have served in the SAS, discovered a lost city in the sands of Arabia, climbed the deadly North Face of the Eiger or summited Everest; but each of us has goals we want to achieve, and our own metaphorical mountains to climb. Sometimes we must learn to pick ourselves up from failure or regret, and go again. We will all lose people we love, and have to deal with that loss. We will all age, and sometimes be afraid, and have moments of self-doubt. We will all be faced with the choice to stop, or to push on to our own Pole and beyond. It is my hope that this collection of stories from my career, studded throughout with lessons learned the hard way in my own life, might help you to get there.

But first things first. Before you can strap on your skis, desert boots or climbing crampons, you need to decide what you're aiming for in life.

CHAPTER ONE

▲

FIND YOUR MOUNTAIN

Try chewing a few prawns before you announce to the
world that you intend to devour an entire lobster.

Ranulph Fiennes

▲

What will drive you on

when things get tough?

———

From an early age, the metaphorical mountain that I would aim to climb stood clearly before me. My father died in the Second World War, on the Allies' long push through Italy in 1943, just four months before I was born. Growing up, I was extremely proud of my father's military career and was determined that I would, in due course, command the Royal Scots Greys cavalry regiment as he had done. My life's path unfurled before me. Twenty years after the war I joined the Greys in Germany as an eighteen-year-old lieutenant fresh from Eton.

Whatever glorious vision I might have had of military life, I soon found that tank exercises grinding through the mud and pine forests south of Hamburg were repetitive and uninspiring, despite the menacing presence of overwhelming Soviet tank forces not far to the east. I needed something more stimulating and competitive. The regiment's Colonel agreed that I could start training canoeing, cross-country skiing and orienteering teams to compete in Army races. We won a few trophies and avoided quite a few tank exercises. I began to notice which soldiers were trustworthy, excelled at twisting officers around their little fingers, and could endure hardship without complaint, and which ones were liable to cause trouble. Looking back, it's clear that I was already demonstrating an aptitude for leadership.

The sad truth about peacetime tank manoeuvres was that the officers who got on faster in their careers were those who played by the book. There was no place for individual brilliance or initiative, largely because we were expecting and training for a short, sharp nuclear war.

Above: My father, leading the Royal Scots Greys.

Below: The author, aged twenty, with his Cold War troop.

After three years I volunteered to join the SAS Regiment, and on the day I received my SAS wings I became the youngest captain in the British Army. However, a few months later I was demoted back to lieutenant and sent back to the Scots Greys. My crime had been to use Army plastic explosives to blow up a 20th Century Fox film set in Dorset, which an old friend of mine objected to on environmental grounds. Neither the SAS nor the Army Board were thrilled with this initiative, and my lifelong aspiration to command the Greys suffered a severe setback.

Back in Germany we carried on practising endless retreats from the Soviet border. This was 1967, and at the age of twenty-three I felt old and as if I was going nowhere fast. I needed a new challenge.

▲

A Greys captain serving in Arabia sent me a letter with a colourful stamp. 'Come and join me,' he suggested. 'No tanks, no mud and good pay.' He failed to mention that the Sultan of Oman, his boss, was involved in an escalating war with Marxist revolutionaries.

My application for the posting was approved and, after a quick London course in Arabic (which I failed), I was sent to Muscat in Oman and thence south to the war zone of Dhofar. The Marxist terrorists, who were at home in the jungle-clad Dhofari ravines, had received their training and automatic weapons from the Soviets. Their members far exceeded our puny Sultanate forces and they gained control of the mountains in western Dhofar during my first summer there.

There were no helicopters. The Sultan's entire air force in Dhofar consisted of two antiquated Piston Provost fighters flown by ex-RAF pilots. Our entire navy consisted of a simple wooden dhow. The Scots Greys officer whose letter had attracted me to Arabia was shot through the shoulder in an ambush. His painful evacuation on the back of a mule took eight hours.

The reconnaissance platoon I was to lead was a rag-tag band of thirty men and five dilapidated, open-top Land Rovers. My dream of leading the Greys was receding ever more rapidly, but I concentrated on keeping my focus on the present and the immediate task ahead.

My initiation to being shot at, and the sphincter-tightening experience of driving through minefields, quickly dissipated the lust for excitement that had first drawn me to Oman. When selecting the next challenge, whatever field of work you are in, a key question must always be one of motivation. What deeper meaning can you find that will drive you on when things get tough? It was clear that I needed a just cause to work for if I was to stick my neck out and do a good job in Dhofar. A mercenary captain, Peter Southward-Heyton, supplied me with the information needed to stiffen my spine.

'In Germany, Ran, you were a tiny cog in the vast NATO wheel, but down in Dhofar you can personally make a difference to history. I'm not exaggerating. The Soviets desperately need to control the Omani coast and thus block eighty per cent of the free world's oil. Now they've taken Aden, Dhofar will be next. They will have a brief window of opportunity when this will be easy for them. This year and next. Why? Because all Oman wants freedom from the Sultan. He is undeniably reactionary. No schools, no hospitals. But soon, maybe in a year, his son Qaboos, who is half-Dhofari, will take over. He will be progressive and the people will love him. This will jerk the enemy's propaganda platform from under their feet.

'So,' he continued, 'they must move now in Dhofar. They know that. Great quantities of arms, ammunition and trained cadres are infiltrating as we speak. We will have only one infantry regiment and your mobile platoon in the whole of Dhofar. Anything you can do this year to delay the enemy's consolidation, and their preparations to expel the Sultan from Dhofar, will be vital.'

Buoyed up by Peter's speech, I blitzed the platoon, replacing poor performers with good soldiers that I tempted away from the other three companies when their officers were away on leave. I raised the platoon strength to thirty, including five good drivers who rejuvenated our vehicles. I 'borrowed' eight extra light machine guns, a mortar, grenades and better clothing from a friendly quartermaster.

I was summoned by the Colonel. News from Dhofar was all bad, including a rocket ambush that had wiped out the vehicles and many men of the recce platoon whose patrol sector I was due to take over.

'You must train your men immediately,' the Colonel told me, 'to operate on foot as well as in your Land Rovers.'

For two months, in the heat of the Omani summer, we trained on foot, by day and by night, both on the gravel plains and in the dense scrub of the Jebel Akhdar at 10,000 feet above sea level. Many of the men, exhausted, transferred back to the companies. I found replacements of a tougher disposition.

My training methods were not, so far as I knew, present in any military textbook. They stemmed from common-sense reactions to the emergency situations likely to occur in Dhofar. I remembered from SAS days that movement by night is usually preferable, silence is vital, unpredictability essential, and small units a bonus. We practised night move-ment and hand signals repeatedly, ambush reactions daily, and accurate shooting with live rounds weekly. I read vari-ous guerrilla warfare manuals, sent by mail order, and found Chairman Mao's advice the most sensible and easy to follow.

Boiled down: shout 'Attack! Attack!' and throw a smoke-spilling white phosphorus grenade if you need to retreat, and shout 'Retreat!' when you want to go forwards. Always keep the opposition guessing.

Always keep the opposition guessing.

At the end of the Omani date harvest, we took our leave of northern Oman and drove the five Land Rovers south for 500 miles.

▲

The Rubh al Khali, or Empty Quarter, is the greatest sand desert in the world and stretches for a thousand miles from the Omani coast into Saudi Arabia. In it there is nothing permanent. The eastern fingers of the sands, through which we travelled, stretched flat and grey to the sea, with a surface of black gravel and yellow pans of gypsum.

For a while we patrolled only to the north of the Qara Mountains, which stretch across the length of Dhofar, separating the arid northern deserts from the fertile plain of Salalah to the south. In Salalah village the Sultan lived in a whitewashed palace overlooking the Indian Ocean.

White sand and oases of coconut palms led away west and east from the palace as far as the eye could see. The Marxist-controlled Qara mountains rose sheer from the plain only eight miles to the north of the palace. The mountains themselves, though hundreds of miles in length, were but ten miles across between southern plain and northern deserts.

Army strength in Dhofar numbered fewer than 300 men, whereas some 4,000 armed terrorists held the mountains. To drive over the only vehicle track that crossed the Qara was a

---

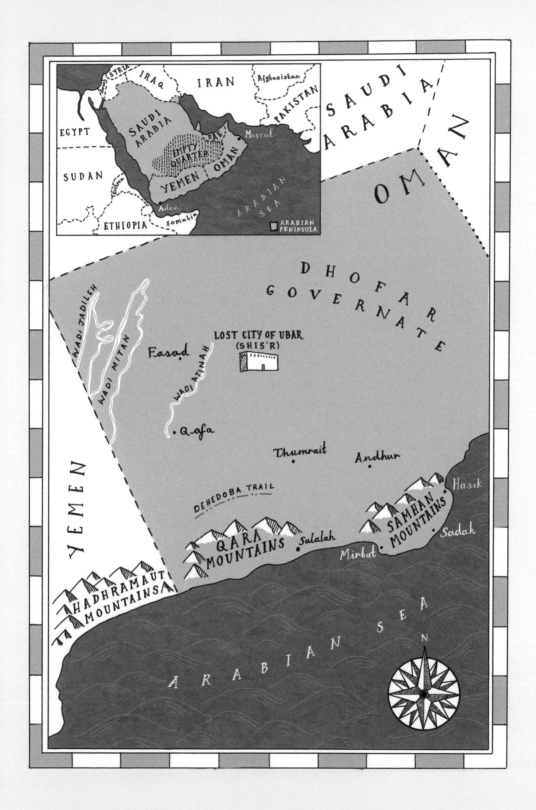

lethal experience involving mines and ambush, but we were lucky. Once on Salalah plain we began a series of ambushes, moving only by night to hide in caves and deep forest. We could usually carry enough ammunition and water for four days.

We killed many of the enemy, had many near scrapes, and lived in constant fear of mines – both the tank mines that could throw a Land Rover thirty yards and the anti-personnel devices which blew your foot through your stomach and removed your face. There were snakes everywhere. The carpet viper's venomous bite could render a strong man brain-dead in seconds. Seven-inch-long camel spiders and the even bulkier, poison-fanged wolf spiders were common.

Hyenas and wolves roamed the foothills, leopards and wild cats snarled from caves, and ticks, whose bite paralysed or poisoned, dropped on to passers-by from foliage. Twelve-inch centipedes, great scorpions and giant lizards scuttled about as we lay 'doggo' in ambush hides. A great place for nature lovers.

I always led from the front, mainly because
I knew where I wanted to go and how
fast a pace I needed to set.

At night the stars were huge as we advanced in a long, silent file, sometimes with a guide, but more often using highly inaccurate maps. Patrick Brook, an old Army friend, was ambushed in the hills one day and a bullet smashed the flask he carried on his right hip. Another drilled through his left arm. The soldiers immediately ahead of and behind him were killed. His guardian angel was on top form that day.

Twin fortresses face each other, almost at spitting distance, across the Yemeni border.

I always led from the front, mainly because I knew where I wanted to go and how fast a pace I needed to set. I found it impossible to convey these wishes to anyone else.

Some officers wore comfortable clothes and shaved. They stood out like sore thumbs – prime targets for enemy snipers. Nearly all my men wore standard Army camouflage. I tried to dress exactly like them in order to increase my chances of survival.

In exchange for information about enemy movements, we gave food and medicine to the goat-herds in the valleys. They would ask when we would next visit so that they could tell other sick people to come. Suspecting they might tell the enemy, we readied ourselves for any would-be ambushers, but sometimes we grew tired and careless. On two such occasions we nearly paid with our lives.

I learned that wherever we moved, by day or by night, I must observe every feature we passed. The sudden terror of an ambush could numb the brain. Instant reaction was crucial, and possible only by knowing the whereabouts of the nearest cover – immediately.

Many of the world's greatest mountaineers have died on their way back down from hazardous ascents. Exhausted, they had dropped their guard. In Dhofar I learned never to relax within a war zone. No operation was over, no matter how successful it appeared, until every man was safely back in base. The same is true in any challenging moments we might face in life: continue to expect and plan for the worst, keep your resolve high, and don't relax your focus until you are well through and out the other side.

For months we lived on the move in the scorching gravel deserts, dodging enemy traps, suffering ulcerating desert sores, straying many miles over the Yemeni border and never developing a routine. The key was always to respect the enemy, but never to allow that respect to overawe and blunt the scope of our own strategy.

I could sense when the recce men were on edge, though they seldom complained. The hardest times were the month of Ramadan, when no Muslim should eat or drink during daylight hours. When we needed to move quickly by day, with heavy loads in the searing heat, it was doubly wearisome to fast. Since the Koran was inflexible, I decided to follow the same rules as the men. That way I could ask more from them without fear of the attitude, 'It's all right for him, he's not fasting.' Experiencing the privations of Ramadan for myself also greatly increased my already considerable respect for the innate toughness of the men.

My unofficial adviser in Oman was also one of my veteran corporals, Mohammed Rashid. Although we met only on active duty, I knew he was always honest about what he felt I should or should not have done or said. I valued his advice. One of his dictums has stood me in good stead ever since. 'Those who talk too much will never guard a secret,' he said. 'They would do better to keep silent so that their shortcomings lie hidden. Then they may pass as wise men. God blessed us with two ears but only one tongue. We should speak therefore half what we hear.'

In October that year I was summoned by the Sultan's Intelligence Officer to penetrate deep into the eastern headquarters of the enemy and kidnap two key political commissars. The subsequent operation, code-named Operation Snatch, was the most hazardous of my Army life but, in a small way, it made up for my failure to achieve my life's dream – the command of the Royal Scots Greys.

Our ambush was eventually a success but, to avoid being shot at close range myself, I had to kill both the commissars. We removed all the documents that they carried, from which

▲

Speak half what you hear,
and you will hear more.

———

Intelligence learned a great deal about the enemy's organisation. Many names and ranks of their leaders were revealed, along with their intended policy.

More importantly, the death of the two commissars, in the centre of their stronghold, had far-reaching effects on the enemy morale at a key period. Tribesmen, hitherto cowed by the Marxists, fled to the government safe havens for the first time and asserted themselves as anti-Communist Muslims. The enemy was wrong-footed at the crucial moment when, a few months after our operation, the Sultan was overthrown, with British complicity, and his progressive son Qaboos took over. It was during those key months, prior to the coup, when both Dhofar and northern Oman were ripe for revolution, that the enemy could have struck with force and sparked off a general uprising.

That they did not seize the opportunity was largely due to their uncertainty as to the mountain tribesmen's loyalty, an uncertainty first promoted by the informers who led us to kill the commissars.

▲

The day that I left the men of the recce platoon, somewhere in the wilderness of the Dehedoba trails, was one I shall never forget. I counted many of them as true friends.

Service regulations were such that I could no longer stay with the Army. The problem went back to my inability to pass the A-level exams necessary to enter the Sandhurst Military Academy and obtain a regular commission. There was a time when one could get an officership without A-levels, but the British Army had moved on. I reckon a person is intelligent to a certain degree, and I began to realise that my capacity wasn't sufficient to become Colonel of the Regiment. After eight years of service, I could sign on no more and was forced to become a civilian.

Twenty-six is quite old to start out in life with no qualifications and a lifelong ambition in ruins. I had no business connections and no sure idea of any particular career goal. But I had developed no little self-reliance in my time in Oman, and knew that I was capable of being a strong, decisive leader. I knew that I was resourceful, street-smart if not book-smart, and highly motivated to find a new purpose in life.

As I look back on my young self now, what advice would I give him in facing this apparent setback? To do the same again, without hesitation. In truth, I have never really suffered from regrets. All that has happened, good as well as bad, is spilt milk, nothing more, and my only advice is just to get on with it. Besides, there is sweetness there too in the wreckage of my ambition to lead the Greys, which I can perhaps only see in hindsight. These formative experiences nudged me towards what would become my life's work, journeying the world and raising millions of pounds for good causes. And I was about to meet someone special, a soulmate with whom to shape a new ambition together. As Shackleton might have said, Lady Luck – whom he called 'Provi', short for Providence – would come my way in due course.

CHAPTER TWO

▲

AMBITION

Nothing will ever be attempted if all possible objections
must first be overcome.

Samuel Johnson

Life is too short
to waste time on
second-class ambitions.

Under the great khaki umbrella that is the British Army, I had enjoyed great stability in my life and every reasonable need had been met. Now I was on my own. I spoke German, French and Arabic quite well, so perhaps I could work in Intelligence. I applied to MI6, was interviewed and turned down. No specific reason was ever given.

My girlfriend Ginny decided to help. We had been neighbours in Sussex since she was nine, and during my leave from Dhofar the previous year she had helped to organise a journey up the Nile, the longest river in the world, by mini-hovercraft, along with two of my Scots Greys friends.

On a whim, Ginny had visited Britain's best-known literary agent for expedition writers, George Greenfield, and she decided that I should write a book about the Nile expedition, on the basis of which, to my great surprise and delight, George took me on as a client. On my return from Dhofar I produced the text in good time, and the royalties totalled £450, which was enough to keep me going for several months, so long as I lived a frugal life at my mother's house in Sussex.

Five months after leaving the Army I was still receiving negative responses to all my job applications, and in desperation I began to give lectures at local town halls using colour slides of the Nile expedition. Slowly I infiltrated the town-hall network and, since Britain then had an inexhaustible supply of town halls paying lecturers £18 inclusive of travel costs, I was unlikely to end up on the dole.

Expedition lectures were easy to give, so, all in all, I decided that, for the future, expeditions might well provide a viable format for self-employment. Ginny and I soon began

Above: Locals inspect one of our hovercraft on our
Nile expedition.

Below and opposite: Exploring the Briksdalsbre and
Fabergstolsbre glaciers in Norway.

work on my first 'professional' expeditions, skiing over a high glacial drift route in Norway and a long journey down the rivers of Canada by boat, and the die was cast. I would do this for a living.

I was also ready to move on to a more ambitious expedition still: marrying Ginny two weeks after our return from Norway.

I remember making it clear to her that I wanted to marry her; I just didn't necessarily want to fix a date for it. Ginny was clear in her response: here's your ring back, and let me know when you've made up your mind. In the end, it was an old Army friend, Patrick Brook, who got me across the line. When Ginny asked his advice after another of my proposals, he spoke frankly. 'Well, this new expedition to Norway is so dangerous, he's likely to die anyway, so you might as well say yes.'

I promised we'd get married within two weeks of my return from Norway, and we did.

▲

It all began one glorious Highland day lazing on the beach of one of the lonely isles of Loch Garve. The sun was warm, falcons wheeled overhead and the cry of the plovers fitted in to my daydreams.

'Why don't we leave London and spend our lives travelling – away from the rat race?' Ginny sat up. I only grunted, so she threw sand on me. 'Seriously, why don't we go round the world? Life is short and we've already wasted quite enough of it in London.'

'Everyone goes round the world these days.'

'No, I mean *properly* round the world. On its axis. Through the Poles – both of them. Keeping more or less to the same Meridian all the way.'

'It's an excellent idea but I doubt it could be done. You'd have to cross the Arctic and Antarctic. You'd need massive back-up, dozens of people, mountains of money . . .'

Ginny was adamant. If this were to be our chosen line of business, we must never waste time planning expeditions that somebody, anybody, had ever done before. We must be the first humans, not merely the first British, to 'get there'. Such a policy would, of course, mean that our failure rate would be high: to believe otherwise would be unrealistic and conceited.

I could think of many individuals who had achieved what we were after – explorers who mapped new territory, and Cook, Columbus and Livingstone were obvious examples. Paraphrasing a great quotation by the writer André Gide: The thing is so difficult it is not worth attempting. The thing is so difficult I cannot help attempting it.

Put another way, life is too short to waste time on second-class ambitions. Go for the big ones, even if that means a higher failure rate. This is surely true for any life, no matter your background or abilities. At some point in any career, a normally unjustifiable risk might need to be taken to make the quantum leap from the mediocre to the big time.

But time was running out, and within three or four years high-orbiting satellites would scan and map the last hidden jungles and ice-caps of the world. We might in the 1970s still be just in time if we put our skates on. We might still go where no human had trod.

Together, Ginny and I traced out the idea of circumnavigating the Earth, without flying one inch of the way, on a six-inch globe. Using reference books, we confirmed that nobody had yet done such a journey. We would need an ice-breaker, a resupply ski-plane, and some £29-million-worth of sponsorship to stand the remotest chance of success. At that time we had £210 in the bank, a semi-detached house near Hammersmith Bridge, and a Jack Russell terrier.

Nonetheless, if we were to progress from the ongoing mediocrity of run-of-the-mill expeditions to truly innovative projects, we must go soon for a make-or-break challenge. The Transglobe Expedition was therefore launched on paper in early 1973, and was to involve both of us full-time for the next ten years. Over that period we descended to and hovered around the breadline, for all our energies were focused on the venture, leaving minimal time to earn a living.

At the beginning we decided that we would retain sole leadership of the project and we would never pay anybody anything at any time. Even the smallest item must be sponsored. To ensure this rule was never broken, we opened neither bank account nor credit facility.

We needed – at no cost – an office, a phone, and a large storage facility in central London, so I approached my Territorial SAS Regiment's colonel.

Would the SAS sponsor the expedition? Would they give us an office and store at their barracks near Sloane Square? Because of my indiscretion with explosives six years before, the SAS boss, Peter de la Billière, agreed to the sponsorship only on the condition that the SAS Colonel who had sacked me from the regular SAS should now become the official overseer of the Transglobe project. This was agreed, and at once we began working from an attic office in the barracks.

The meticulous polar research work, mostly in London and Cambridge, took us a year. The only feasible route, it transpired, was to follow, as closely as possible, the longitudinal line 0°/180°, known as the Greenwich Meridian. From Greenwich we would travel south to Antarctica. After crossing Antarctica via the South Pole, the route headed north up the Pacific, past Fiji, to Canada's west coast. When ice in the

With Ginny, never happier than when poring over maps,
planning our next adventure.

Bering Straits blocked the way, we would jink east up the Yukon and Mackenzie rivers, through the Northwest Passage, and over the Arctic Ocean via the North Pole. Thence, back down to Greenwich.

If all went well everywhere and there were no delays, we might be able to complete the journey in just over three years. However, we based all our plans on bad weather conditions.

We approached over 3,000 companies in London during the first two years. By 1975, 760 of them had agreed to provide us with their goods or services. To persuade the reluctant hard-headed businessmen to give us many millions of pounds' worth of support for a project that looked nigh-on impossible required the basic arts of the salesman. These arts I rapidly acquired. As a leader, it is my belief that whenever feasible, you should pick your team on character, not skill. You can teach skills. You can't alter character. The same is true for you: if you have the motivation, then you can do the work to fill any skill gap you might have.

You can teach skills.
You can't alter character.

After seven years' full-time work we obtained the full £29 million of hardware, including such items as a forty-two-year-old ice-strengthened ship, a resupply ski-plane and £2-million-worth of fuel to be delivered to various remote points around the world.

The biggest obstacle by far, and one which did often seem insuperable, was bureaucracy. The Foreign Office had never given any private expedition their blessing to go to Antarctica. Only government-approved operations had ever been there since, but without assistance with fuel for resupply, no Pole journey would be feasible. Only the United States South Pole Authority could grant this, and, without an official request from the Foreign Office, they would never do so. The Foreign Office would not move a muscle without the blessing of the Royal Society, and the Royal Society would not consider us without the prior approval of our plans by the British Antarctic Survey.

Private British expeditions wanting to go to Antarctica were naturally anathema to the British Antarctic Survey. They considered the frozen continent to be their territory and did their level best to preserve it from all irresponsible (meaning non-British Antarctic Survey) outsiders. To date, they had a 100 per cent success rate.

For four years, despite maintaining an almost constant stream of requests, I was steadfastly turned down. Antarctica was a no-go area and would remain so unless I could somehow break through the rock-steady bureaucratic defences.

I fared no better in terms of the Arctic Ocean sector, although in this region the Foreign Office was luckily not involved. In order to mount any expedition to the North Pole, never mind to cross the entire ocean, it was necessary to set out from remote Ellesmere Island in Canada. I could not hope to fly all the necessary equipment to the northern edge of Ellesmere without help from the RAF (who flew empty transport planes on exercises to nearby Greenland).

After four years of soul-destroying attacks on the various authorities, north and south, I had to admit temporary defeat. I wrote then to all our sponsors to explain why the expedition was being postponed until 1978. This would give me two years' grace before renewing the attack but, by now, Ginny and I were in penury, as were the other volunteers in the barracks office.

During the first two years, we had merely tried to put the project on a war footing; to turn it from a dream into a feasible reality. After all, any human being, however meek they might think themselves, can nurture a single-minded desire to fulfil a particular goal. The quantum leap is the moment of instigation, that first push to make the stone roll. Thereafter all manner of unforeseen outside factors will fall into place, and the very act of starting will shift quite a few of the apparent obstacles. In the words of the Scots philosopher William Murray, 'The moment one definitely commits oneself, then Providence moves too. All sorts of things then happen that would otherwise never have occurred.'

The quantum leap is the moment of instigation, that first push to make the stone roll.

We all dream of the things we want to achieve in our short lives, but once you have articulated that ambition, you could do worse than to ask yourself: *what is that first push to make the stone roll?* What is stopping you, other than simply starting?

As my great friend Mike Stroud wrote many years later, about our bid to run seven marathons on seven continents in seven days together (see Chapter 9):

'Whereas most people look at very big challenges, whatever the field or their walk of life, and start from the position "I can't", Ran and I make a simple word substitution and say "Why can't I?" "I can't run seven marathons" easily transforms into the question, "Why can't I run seven marathons?" Once it was asked, we felt obliged to find the answer.'

CHAPTER THREE

▲

TEAMWORK

No man is an Island, entire of itself.

John Donne

▲

When you bury
the hatchet, make sure
the handle is not left
above ground.

———

To take *friends* on stressful expeditions has always seemed to me to be foolish, since I can think of no easier way of marring a friendship for ever. An expedition's aim is best achieved by individuals who can look after themselves, need little or no directing or nursing, and are tough in body and mind. I look for professional and dogged people, and treat any friendship resulting from an expedition as an unexpected bonus.

Polar expeditions are well known for causing stress and enmity between participants, and quite why my teammates and I have never come to blows, literally or even verbally, during our Arctic and Antarctic journeys, remains a mystery to me.

The fewer people in a team the better, is my general rule.

Since the idea of Transglobe was for a small group to travel from Greenwich, through both Poles, and back to Greenwich, without flying one yard of the entire three-year route, I knew we would need two or three very special individuals. The fewer people the better is my general rule, since human beings are quite badly designed for getting on with each other when under stress. How to choose them? I have always believed that if you are to be held responsible for other people's safety, then you must check them out as thoroughly as you would your own child.

On most expeditions under pressure, a 'them and us' attitude will develop, something I learned the hard way some

Working together to find a route through thick pack-ice
en route to the North Pole, 1986.

years before Transglobe, on an unprecedented 3,000-mile boat journey through Canada, from the Yukon river down the length of British Columbia to the American border. Such conflict can be destructive if it lowers the ability of the team to progress, though as with my journey across Antarctica with Mike Stroud, some simmering tension can also act as a powerful distraction from the difficulty of the challenge itself. But from a television film director's point of view, such stresses and strains can make wonderful viewing. I had once watched a TV film of a sailor taking a cramped yacht crew around the world. A two-man film crew had stirred up resentment on board expressly, it seemed, to highlight antagonisms and spice up their film. I was aware that the BBC might try this in Canada, and the warning signs were not slow in surfacing.

I well remember a day of forked lightning and impressive whirlpools when we were all tense with apprehension. A first attempt to ram the boats upstream through a formidable series of rapids had failed. I knew we must deflate the smaller boat and carry it through forests, but the TV crew were against it and the soldiers travelling with me conducted a silent mutiny of inaction. Darkness was nigh, and non-stop rain would swell the river overnight, so there was no time for patient discussion. I began to deflate the small boat myself, and one by one the men joined me to help.

In an action situation, I believe, there is no better way out of many deadlocks than for the leader to get on with the job himself (or herself) and, where feasible, simply to ignore the arguments and inactivity of the dissenting parties. Sometimes it is clearly best for an expedition leader to lay down the law

Negotiating fierce rapids on the Fraser river with Stan Cribbett.

and then stick to it through thick and thin, ignoring any muttering in the ranks. But, so long as it does not endanger life or the long-term aims of the expedition, a middle course of diplomatic appeasement is more useful. The skill is in knowing when to choose which tactic.

Canada taught me a valuable lesson. When you are looking for your team, always presume the worst. If the candidates really want to come onto a particular expedition, they will tell you any old corkers because, quite rightly, they have a strong desire, and will say what they need to get it.

Indeed, on our earlier Norwegian expeditions we *had* the worst. They all said they could climb, but no one – including myself – had ever climbed before. On every subsequent expedition I instituted 'the black talk', which I gave to every applicant as soon as he or she volunteered. This was a pessimistic summary of all the dreadful scenarios that might possibly occur en route. When things go badly – perhaps dangerously – wrong, the team will be less angry with their leader if he argued the case for his actions up-front and painted a negative picture of likely outcomes which, after the setback, he can regurgitate. As an added bonus, however, the black talk also served as an excellent weeding-out process for less than deeply committed individuals.

Always be direct, and plan for the worst possible conditions.

A blunt approach to setting the conditions for a successful team on an expedition is essential, but there is something to learn here for any working group, or indeed any friendship or relationship. Always be direct, and plan for the worst possible conditions. If the sun is shining, pack a raincoat. All the better if the sun continues to shine, but at least together you are prepared.

▲

For the much more ambitious Transglobe project, I asked a polar expert, Colonel Andrew Croft, what team number he advised. 'With three men,' he told me, 'two can gang up on the leader. I would suggest that you, as leader, should only decide whether to have two or three colleagues after you have seen them all in action during Arctic training.'

Since nobody would let us in to the Arctic at the time, I decided North Wales would have to do for team selection and training. Each winter weekend for the next three years, the Territorials provided Army trucks and rations for me to train a mountain racing team in Snowdonia and from the team hopefuls, about sixty SAS men in all, I picked the three best ones who applied for the expedition.

Many expeditions, I knew, had foundered through internal schisms brought about by their top-heavy make-up – lots of expert specialists all jostling for position. Selection through skills alone could easily end up with big trouble in the ranks. A team of this ilk might typically include a doctor, a mechanic, a navigator, a radio operator, a scientist or two, and, most troublesome of all, a cameraman and film crew. In short, a nest of prima donnas and ingredients likely to curdle.

Better, surely, to search for conventional people with everyday jobs who stand up well to three criteria: level-headedness, patience, and good nature towards others.

By early 1976 we had narrowed the search to two men: Charlie Burton, a retired corporal from the Sussex Regiment and by then a security officer; and Oliver Shepard, a beer salesman. Neither had expedition experience, but both

Oliver Shepard (left) and
Charlie Burton (below).

seemed suitable personality-wise, being patient and lacking that all-too-common human complaint of malice, which surfaces easily in small, confined communities. (As an aside, if you know that you have a rotten apple in your team, get rid of it sooner, not later.)

Look for three things: level-headedness, patience, and good nature towards others.

I wanted men who could look after themselves in extreme conditions, possessed plenty of creative energy and initiative, and would normally be selected as leaders in whatever field of activity they chose. Yet a paradox clearly presented itself here, because any leader will find life a lot easier with natural 'yes-men' rather than a bunch of individualists with a tendency to question any suggested course of action.

▲

In 1977 Colonel Andrew Croft helped me attract a number of key individuals to form an expedition committee. Sir Vivian Fuchs, who had led the first and only crossing of Antarctica, kindly joined and became pivotal to our ongoing progress. As were Dr John Heap of the Polar Desk at the Foreign Office, and Dr Charles Swithinbank of the British Antarctic Survey. Wally Herbert, who ten years earlier had led the first and only crossing of the Arctic Ocean, became a valued critic and adviser. All of these men urged us to gain experience in the Arctic and Greenland before attempting Transglobe.

Following their advice and obtaining the necessary extra sponsorship, we spent an additional year in Greenland and the Arctic Ocean learning about the unique obstacles those regions present to the would-be traveller. On our return we

---

spoke with new confidence, and our advisers took us more seriously. Now they were prepared to risk their own names to push our case with the authorities. Slowly, very slowly, official doors began to show chinks of daylight.

We learned that the snowfields that cover the Antarctic and Greenland land masses present very different obstacles compared to the sea-ice that floats on the Arctic Ocean. Tests of our existing snow machines during our trials revealed many misconceptions just in time for me to find sponsors for a different type of snowmobile capable of working at both ends of the world.

Our three-man group would travel by ship over the oceans, by Land Rover in Africa's deserts and jungles, by snowmobile in Antarctica, by twelve-foot rubber boat on Canadian rivers and through the Northwest Passage, on foot, ski and snowshoe over Ellesmere Island, and by ski, snowmobile and canoe over the Arctic Ocean.

To resupply us over the vast polar ice-tracts I signed up two superb ski-plane pilots, one British and one Swiss. The ship's crew consisted of fourteen volunteers from eight countries, each of whom gave up their existing careers to join us for a minimum of three years' unpaid service.

Knowing nothing about ships, we initially advertised in a shipping magazine for a volunteer crew, and the first applicant who we liked the look of was told to find a ship, crew and all relevant equipment, at no cost, in eighteen months. Anton Bowring, previously a deliverer of small craft made in Suffolk, took on this task with two volunteer helpers. By September 1978 things looked sufficiently hopeful, after six years' work, to announce a departure date from Greenwich in twelve months' time.

We now had twenty-five unpaid individuals working full-time, often round the clock, and over 1,900 sponsor companies.

As yet we had spent no money at all on the venture, only time and effort.

I kept a tight control, along the lines of Chairman Mao's five-year plans, but adding the ingredient of realism to the activities of each team member. Every three weeks I called the team to the barracks office and ran through the action lists delegated to each person to see who had or had not yet done his or her outstanding tasks. The idle ones were shown up in front of the others, and any dangerous signs of unreadiness were focused on immediately. This was designed to avoid a last-minute panic.

Exactly six years after I first began to harass the Foreign Office I finally received their guarded approval for the Antarctic phase, and the Canadian government's seal of approval for the Arctic.

The idle ones were shown up in front of the others, and any dangerous signs of unreadiness were focused on immediately.

Seven long years after the date of Ginny's suggestion, we set out from Greenwich with our Patron, HRH The Prince of Wales, at the ship's helm. To the crowd of many thousands of well-wishers Charles said: 'Transglobe is one of the most ambitious undertakings of its kind ever attempted, and the scope of its requirements is monumental. Even though a decade has passed since man set foot on the Moon, polar exploration and research remains as important as ever. As this great journey unfolds, I am confident that this courageous undertaking will provide interest and inspiration to young and old alike throughout the world.' The *New York*

Times editorial that day stated: 'The British aren't so weary as they are sometimes said to be. The Transglobe Expedition leaves Greenwich, England, today on a journey of such daring that it makes one wonder how the sun ever set on the empire.'

▲

Of course, the one key team member I have not mentioned yet, is myself. I have always been highly motivated and naturally found myself in the role of leader in many of my expeditions, but on one memorable occasion it was clear that I would need to take my old Omani colleague Mohammed Rashid's advice to speak less, and start to listen.

Casting around for a new challenge to push me to my limits in the early 2000s, at some point I had tentatively approached Alpine climbing expert Kenton Cool with the suggestion that, if the Eiger was famously said to be a tougher challenge, exposure-wise, than Everest, would he guide me up it? And if so, when? I knew that Kenton had climbed the North Wall of the Eiger with two friends and had taken three days and nights to do so. I also knew that he was held in huge respect by Britain's mountaineering community. He was thirty-three years old and supremely fit. He lived and worked in Chamonix, the Mecca of Alpine climbers, and did not suffer fools, especially climbing fools, gladly. In response to my Eiger query, he was forthright. He would not even consider climbing the Eiger with me unless he first taught me how to climb to a standard where he was sure that he would not be risking his own life.

How long would such an instructional period last, I asked him. 'As long,' he replied, 'as a piece of string. It depends on your ability, determination, strength, and how long you're prepared to spend training in the Alps. Have you read *The White Spider?*'

'No,' I replied.

'Well, you probably should. It may put you off before you even think of going anywhere near the Eiger.'

I found a copy of the book, written by the Austrian Heinrich Harrer, one of the team who made the first ascent back in 1938, and I noted his description of 'the indescribable labours and difficulties' of the climb that 'demand the uttermost physical, spiritual and mental resistance'. *The White Spider* made harrowing reading and explained in detail the reasons for many of the deaths of the highly capable climbers who perished on the North Face. I was impressed and not a little disturbed. But from the point of view of a worthy vertigo-testing challenge, the mountain seemed perfect.

I went back to Kenton, who agreed to have a go at teaching me how to climb on mixed rock and ice in the Alps. The basics of ice-climbing, as far as I could see, involved hacking one or both of your axes into the ice-wall above your head, kicking the front-facing spikes on your boots into the ice at about knee-level, then hauling your weight up. You then keep repeating this process until you reach the top.

An American climbing journal sent a freelance journalist, Greg Child, out to Chamonix to record a typical Kenton training day. Greg had himself been a world-renowned mountaineer for many years. 'We're all clammy with sweat when we reach the frozen waterfall,' he wrote. 'Ropes uncoiled, ice-axes leashed to wrists, and crampons clamped to boots. "Baron von Cool" (Ran's pet name for his guide) leads us up a swathe of vertical ice. Ran hacks with his ice-axes and Cool pulls the rope in on his waist. Despite his mangled hand and awkward grip, Ran swings his ice tool true and confidently, and judging by our relaxed banter, he's well on his way to conquering his lifelong fear of heights. Cool then belays me up. I find that the cold air has rendered the ice so brittle that grapefruit-size chunks of it are exploding all around me as I hack my ice-axes into the cascade. Halfway up to the ledge where Cool and Ran are seated I notice a trail of blood. The droplets lead straight to Ran's nose, which an ice shard has neatly slit. He's unperturbed, and he sits on his perch with a bloody grin.

'With Cool in the lead, we start up a rambling ice-wall near Italy's Cogne Valley, a Grade 4+ named Patri. Mini tornadoes of powder-snow sting us whenever the wind feels angry. On a low-angled stretch of the route, Ran steps on the rope in his spiked boots – a climbing no-no.

'"Get off that bloody thing, Ran," Cool barks like a rabid drill sergeant.

'Ran smiles at me, and steps aside. For an alpha male accustomed to unconditional authority over his expeditions, his deference to Cool is quaint. It's also pragmatic: he knows he's on a learning curve as a climber, and he's soaking up everything Cool can teach.'

▲

There is no single approach to being a good team player, and as we will see in the next chapter, it comes much more naturally to me to be out front on my own. But as you are no doubt beginning to learn about me, above all I value directness and pragmatism, with a hearty dash of humility where required. Sarcasm must be avoided like the plague if a team is to thrive. Bad apples must be tossed aside at the earliest opportunity. And if you find confrontations hard, always remember that an argument usually produces plenty of heat, but little light. Be bold, confront any differences of opinion or disagreements head on – after which the hatchet should be buried and the handle *not* left above ground.

CHAPTER FOUR

▲

LEADERSHIP

Be flexible most of the time, but reserve the option
to be inflexible some of the time.

Ranulph Fiennes

▲

The surest way I know
of 'leading leaders'
is to be entirely
sure of yourself.

———

I am a severe critic of Roland Huntford's openly hostile biography of Captain Scott, but I wholeheartedly agree with his comment that, 'In polar expeditions, as in most tight-knit groups, there is usually a process of selecting a natural or psychological leader. It is a conflict akin to a fight for domination within a wolf pack; a more or less overt challenge to the established, formal leadership. How he deals with this threat to his authority is one of the tests through which most commanders have to go . . .'

The great Norwegian explorer Amundsen clashed tragically with his number two, Hans Johansen – a clash that led eventually to a showdown. Amundsen was forced to be heavy-handed and Johansen, never able to forget the humiliation that followed, finally committed suicide. Shackleton's physical strength was an adjunct of leadership that he did not hesitate to use. When a recalcitrant crewman on his ship refused to obey him, he hit the man repeatedly until he did as he was bidden.

Such tactics have never been part of my armoury, and I have never been tempted to 'get physical' on any expedition. My policy has always been to choose self-reliant, strong characters for my team since they are more likely to push themselves against great odds. The downside of such people is often that they are, in the words of Dr Phillip Law, the famous director of Australia's DEA Antarctic Division, 'fundamentally antagonistic and critically outspoken'. Mike Stroud was of just such a persuasion. He openly disapproved of leadership *per se* and felt strongly that all decisions on an expedition, especially with a small party of only two or three, should be taken by democratic agreement.

Democracy does not come easily to me. I will admit that the only position that I can tolerate on an expedition is that of team leader. In the Army, officers are taught to lead from behind. Amundsen, Steger and many other polar leaders followed this sensible tenet, but I have always led from the front in physical terms, and that involved handling all the navigation and setting a sensible travel pace. I will follow Mike's democratic route (when there is time) of talking about options, rather than pronouncing dictatorial and unilateral decisions. I will listen to advice, patiently discuss criticisms to my suggested course of action and, whenever a better course is suggested, go with it at once and give open credit for it. But if others, whether or not they form a majority, favour an opinion that I believe to be stupid, dangerous, or unlikely to help attain the goal of the expedition, then I will overrule them, no matter how dissatisfied this may make them feel.

Leadership, in such circumstances, must be a careful chairmanship conducting an ongoing system of checks. Over the years, I have slowly learned to keep my antennae alert at all times to the cross-currents of atmosphere, the ever-changing undercurrents of people's moods and topics to be avoided. In isolated conditions under stress, even imagined molehills easily become great mountains and vicious storms blow up in teacups of hurt pride.

I do not believe in relying on a God-given leadership status that will not be challenged. I do believe in constantly looking over my shoulder to ensure any potential challenge to my position is politely, but firmly, seen off. I hold no brief for a split command and, as a great believer in the principle of the thin edge of the wedge, I steer clear of asking

▲

*Under stressful conditions,
even imagined molehills can
easily become great mountains
and vicious storms blow up in
teacups of hurt pride.*

———

for advice since this will usually set a precedent and encourage people to proffer further suggestions when they are not wanted.

▲

As we finally set off on the long-awaited Transglobe journey, making our way steadily to Africa on the first leg of our bid to circle the Earth, I decided to hold a meeting on deck. I ran through the entire three-year plan and outlined the many problems we were likely to face in living together over the years ahead. I stressed that the land group were no more important to the end goal of the venture than were the ship's crew. The whole team must strive to work as one or we would certainly fail in the herculean tasks that lay ahead. I ventured some guidelines of patience, tolerance and selflessness that might help, and suggested that anybody who felt they could not take the set-up on board should feel free to leave at Algiers the next day.

I ventured some guidelines of patience, tolerance and selflessness.

At Abidjan on the Ivory Coast, on the Greenwich Meridian, we again boarded the ship. Her sponsors were C. T. Bowring of London, together with the US partners Marsh & McLennan, and her name was *Benjamin Bowring* or, to all of the crew, simply the *Benji B*.

Our passage from Cape Town to the Antarctic pack-ice was stormbound and the *Benji B* behaved sluggishly, laden as she was with over 1,500 forty-five-gallon drums of fuel and her holds bursting with cargo. Only one man on board, a deckhand, had ever been in Antarctic waters before.

Above: Ollie, RF and Charlie in the forests of the Ivory Coast.

Below: The *Benji B* is greeted by the locals in Antarctica, 1979.

Left: Ginny and Bothie,
summer 1979.

Below: Charlie in
storage tunnel at
Borga Base, 1980.

Unloading in Antarctica was rushed for fear of a storm as we lay against the ice. Everyone had a specific task, sleeping minimally in shifts, for hundreds of tons of equipment, all carefully itemised, numbered and flagged, had to be sledged two miles inland and up a natural ice-ramp.

Once the coastal base was ready, the land group went south through the mountains. We travelled with three snowmobiles towing 1,000-pound sledges and crossed the crevasse-riven Hinge Zone, stopping some 300 miles inland at 6,000 feet above sea level, at the edge of the known world. Over the next three weeks we established a cardboard camp and Giles Kershaw, our ski-plane pilot, made over eighty flights from the coastal dump with enough supplies for the four of us to overwinter for eight months. Throughout this static period, including five months of darkness day and night, we would be cut off from all outside assistance.

The crossing of Antarctica from one side to the other, and unassisted by outside groups, had thus far never yet been achieved. The frozen continent, at 5,500 million square miles, dwarfs the USA.

Unknown to us at the time, a sweepstake was set up in the offices of the New Zealand Antarctic Survey. The polar experts there considered our plan underequipped and our snowmobiles underpowered. They had a map of the continent pinned up with comments appended at appropriate points, such as 'First crevasse accident', and 'Pulled out here by US Rescue Hercules'. Their general view was: 'too far, too high and too cold'.

During that winter of 1980 the winds about our cardboard huts shrieked by at up to 132 mph and the wind chill dropped to minus 130°C. Ginny's pet Jack Russell terrier helped to keep the four of us sane. There were moments of aggravation, some tiffs and arguments, but very few, and Charlie wrote:

'We had worked together closely for a long time. We knew each other's moods and when to lay off. Therefore, the strains were negligible.'

Discipline was hardly necessary, which was just as well since there was no way I could have enforced it, and better no threats at all, than idle ones. Our survival in so isolated a spot depended on each person applying self-discipline. We lived in cardboard huts, under the snow, fuelled by petrol. Fire was an ever-present danger, as was carbon monoxide poisoning from our generators. Slops and lavatory bags for four adults over eight months needed careful and ongoing attention. Hundreds of tons of ever-drifting snow required constant shovelling from escape hatches.

Nobody knows what lies ahead because nobody has been here before.

On 29 October Charlie, Ollie and I said goodbye to Ginny and her dog Bothie, and set out to cross Antarctica. (See map on p. 204.) The temperature was minus 50°C and the wind a steady 20 knots. Our route to reach the Pole lay over 900 miles of ice where no human had ever trodden since the world was created. This we would map, and here, if nowhere else, we would be true explorers.

My diary, ten days into our crossing, recorded: 'Nobody knows what lies ahead because nobody has been here before.' Back in Britain I had asked the Antarctic experts in Cambridge what was known of the region. 'Previous forays into your area,' they had written, 'have been turned back by crevassing, so it seems possible that a lot of the way ahead of you, between 79° and 83° South, may be badly crevassed.'

▲

Better no threats at all,

than idle ones.

———

Above: Charlie leans over a crevasse just outside our camp.

Below: Ollie with theodolite.

This dearth of surface data had made any careful route planning impossible.

For 600 miles in this unexplored zone we recorded the height of the ice surface above sea level using aneroid barometers, thereby mapping this part of Earth for the first time, and Oliver drilled ten-yard ice cores which, analysed later in Cambridge, would tell the scientists how much snow had fallen here over the past twenty-five years.

Vast regions of sastrugi blocked our path – ridges of ice cut out by the prevailing wind and running transverse to the line of our advance. We struggled over this immense ploughed field, against the grain of ice-furrows up to four feet high.

The eighteen-inch skis at the front of our machines jammed in the furrow troughs, as did the heavily laden sledges. We used axes, shovels, manpower and foul language to force each mile of painfully slow progress to the south.

The machines broke down frequently. Springs and bogey wheels shattered and buckled. A supercooled ignition key turned too hard snapped clean off. Oliver, the beer salesman, somehow managed to cope with each successive mechanical trouble.

Navigation was a problem every minute of the day in this featureless land. For 1,200 miles I used the sun, my watch and a compass, with nothing solid to aim at or check against. The problem was compounded by many days of white-out, including the day we finally reached the American research station at the South Pole.

My means of determining our daily position was a theodolite and complex navigation tables. This kit weighed 32 pounds. (In the 1980s I switched to a two-pound plastic sextant, thanks to research work into plastics at low temperatures, and after 1991 I began to use a GPS or satellite positioning device which weighed less than nine ounces, thanks to the advent of polar orbiting satellites.)

We stayed for four days at the South Pole station waiting for Ginny and her radio gear to be flown there by Giles. A merry Christmas, planned by the twelve resident scientists, was only a day away, but we needed every hour if we were to complete the crossing during Antarctica's brief summer season. Each day of delay increased the hazards ahead. Summer was already well advanced. Crevasse bridges, sun-weakened, would be increasingly liable to cave in beneath us.

On 2 March the last ships and aircraft would have to leave Antarctica or risk being marooned there for eight months. After that date our own situation would revert to that of Scott's famous group, with zero possibility of rescue or supply.

I noticed an unusual tension in the tent as we approached the edge of the high plateau. Ahead of us lay a 180-mile cliff-girt chute, the Scott Glacier, which dropped through 9,000 feet of chaotic ice to the coastal edge of Antarctica.

One of the most treacherous zones of this glacier, never previously descended, was its upper rim. A white-out caught us in an area of great instability, so we camped fully aware that a hidden network of trapdoors to oblivion lay all about us. Slits and caverns with inch-thin booby-trap doors, and snow covers hiding dizzy drops of 150 feet and more.

Knowing that a weather change could pin us down for two precious weeks, I decided that delay posed a greater danger than attempting to travel blind.

Ollie was silent when I announced this, but Charlie, to use Ollie's words, 'was very shirty as he thought we should have stayed in the tent and not travelled in the white-out through the crevasse field'. Whenever my decisions appeared to the others to be wrong, Charlie was an excellent weathervane. On this occasion I could see his point. To move through a highly volatile zone, unable to spot the hazards ahead or underfoot, could be described as stupid but, in my opinion, we ran a much greater long-term danger if we lost the race against the onrush of polar winter due to short-term caution.

If I was misunderstood through not fully communicating the logic of my decision, then the fault was doubly mine, since my reason for failing to 'discuss options' was merely the desire to avoid an argument that might not win me the most votes.

In a way my past life had cushioned me from having to explain myself to others, especially the years in the Arab army. The Omanis had accepted my instant decisions and changes of mind without question. Reacting to quick-change military situations such as lethal ambushes did not involve a democratic decision-making process with the men.

But Oliver and Charlie were not accustomed to blindly following orders they could not understand. Neither were they, like the majority of the Navy men with Scott and Shackleton, trained to obey without question. On the contrary, they were strong individualists and leaders of men who disliked being told what to do at the best of times. They expected involvement in planning our moves.

Normally I respected this, and many a joint decision took place over the years between the three of us but, when instant action and reaction was required, I reverted to the one-man-band-ism to which the Army had accustomed me. For one thing, it saved precious time.

As it was, I had developed my own, perhaps maverick, policies, and these did not include having a democratic pow-wow with my companions, however brief, when some imminent hazard demanded a speedy reaction. If I was

Charlie refills the water tank with fresh snow, as the sun returns after a five-month absence.

confident that my way was best, what would be the point of a discussion to listen to other possible ways?

The surest way I know of 'leading leaders', without suffering successive confrontations, is to be entirely sure of yourself and to know that nobody has more experience than you do at the job in hand.

So we broke camp, crept forward and, luckily, the white-out lifted. Charlie, careful never to sound excited about anything, described the subsequent journey: 'The descent was hair-raising, too steep for the sledges which ran down ahead of our skidoos, sometimes wrenching them sideways, even backwards, over wide, droopy snowbridges. Some of these bridges had fracture lines on both sides and were obviously ready to implode at the first excuse. How we made the bottom God only knows.'

Against the expectations of polar pundits in many countries, we made the descent without loss of life and, in nine days, crossed the Ross Ice Shelf to Scott Base on the continent's Pacific Rim. We had traversed the Antarctic continent in sixty-seven days, the first one-way-only crossing of Antarctica ever made.*

▲

Giles, our resupply pilot, was known for his polar expertise and his critical nature, vital to a good polar pilot. Of Transglobe he said that, 'Before they even left London, I really doubted that they would succeed. Their land team are, after all, not professionals at anything. I mean, they have learned to cook in Charlie's case, how to be a mechanic in Ollie's, and in Ginny's case how to be a radio operator. Ran is a good

---

* The Fuchs expedition of 1955–8 was a vehicular traverse by two teams that met up at the Pole.

leader, probably a great leader, but he has had to learn about navigation. The great thing about these four people is their persistence as a group in the face of terrible difficulties in getting across; not their individual abilities.'

Unfortunately, any collective ability we may have developed as a group was soon to be reduced. Oliver's American wife had become very worried about his continued absence in risky places and, after much deliberation, he had regretfully responded to her urgings by agreeing to leave Transglobe.

The committee in London decided to find a replacement for Oliver. Sir Vivian Fuchs and Mike Wingate Gray, the ex-SAS CO, flew to meet us in New Zealand. They were completely against Charlie and me attempting the Arctic as a two-man group. I was equally adamant that Oliver should only be replaced if I found that the two of us alone could not cope.

The committee members looked unimpressed. 'Charlie and I have worked together now for six years,' I added. 'We know each other's limitations and plus points. However well we may know some third person in normal circumstances, he may turn out very differently, given the unique stress of Arctic Ocean travel. Quite apart from any personality interaction between us and such a "third man", his very presence could easily undermine our own mutual compatibility.'

The committee, however, remained doggedly against us attempting the ambitious journey without a third man. In desperation, I did what I always do in such straits – I appealed directly to the boss. In the case of Transglobe, the relevant god was our Patron, HRH The Prince of Wales. Due to the time difference, I had to call him at his Gloucestershire home well after midnight and he sounded groggy. I put the 'third man' problem to him and his response was unequivocal. He was due to visit us in Sydney in a fortnight, and he promised that he would put my point of view strongly to the committee.

It would have been easy for the Prince to suggest that we solve our own problems, but because he did act as final arbiter for the expedition, we were able to sort out such matters in a friendly manner by passing the buck upwards to someone whose judgement we all respected.

Never waste time applying to the boss's assistant if you can go directly to the boss.

By now there were fourteen learned people on the London committee. Captain Scott once said of his own expedition committee: 'Too many cooks spoil the broth, and too many men on the committee are the devil.'

Charlie saw things slightly differently. He wrote: 'Ran runs the show. He is the leader in the field . . . If he wants to do something, he does it, and the committee, they try to change it. I think this is the first time he has had people who feel that they should organise him. This is unfortunate for him and he feels the strain. I can see this.'

We would continue through the final Arctic stage of Transglobe as a two-man group. Sir Vivian Fuchs made it clear that if things went wrong as a result, then, as the leader, the burden of irresponsibility would be entirely mine.

CHAPTER FIVE

▲

WONDER

We carry within us the wonders we seek without us.

Sir Thomas Browne

▲

What excites me is the
challenge itself.

_____

'When I've heard journalists ask you why you do this, you're always saying that you've "got to make a living somehow without A-levels". What about all the beauty, Ran?' Mike Stroud genuinely gets fired up by the wilderness. Even operating at his physical limits, he appreciates coming over the brow of a hill and spotting a magnificent view: the sparkling sea of ice all the way to the horizon, the sublime majesty of valley and mountain. I must admit that I would also think such a view fascinating – as a proposition for the photos that our sponsors will need, or for the plate section of the book of the expedition. Fascinating. Or, as Mike might say ruefully, contemptible.

Nonetheless, this is how I make my living. And though I may not be much of a nature-watcher, I have long since learned that I find wonder elsewhere in my work. Over the years, I have found great meaning in the tens of millions of pounds we have raised for charity – and some of those charities, such as those for cancer and heart conditions, have gone on to touch my own life and those I love. Mike, Ginny and others began to uncover ever more amazing scientific insights from our journeys, and that fired me again. You may not find lilting descriptions of oceans of sand and glittering ice in my books or talks, but that is largely because what excites me is the challenge itself.

I have written elsewhere of the need to keep a lookout for Lady Luck, but the same is true of *meaning*. What fires you up and makes you leap out of bed in the morning? What will motivate you to keep going through life's headwinds?

▲

_____

When fighting the Marxists in Dhofar I had heard the *bedu* talk of Ubar, their name for Irem. My guide told me, 'Irem was the finest city in all Arabia, built like Paradise but destroyed by God.'

Since the dawn of civilisation the keystone of trade between the Phoenician and Muscat sailors was frankincense, which came only from the incense orchards of Dhofar and which for two thousand years was more valuable even than gold. Ubar was the desert watering place from which great caravans of two thousand camels and five hundred men set out on their journey through the Empty Quarter to service the incense markets of the world. On Ptolemy's 150 AD map, no cities are shown in Arabia's south-eastern deserts save for Omanum Emporium, the market of Oman, known to later writers, travellers and the Koran as Ubar, or Irem, city of the lost people of Ad. The Book of Genesis indicates that Ad settled his tribe between the Empty Quarter and the Indian Ocean.

I may not be one for admiring the view, but here was something glorious to fire my imagination.

To say the least, this painted quite a picture in my mind. I was about to be thrown out of the Army, and here, as if on cue, was the mirage of something very special. The Queen of Sheba's lost city. The Atlantis of the Sands. I may not be one for admiring the view, but here was something glorious to fire my imagination. I was determined to find it.

What I could not know is that it would take up over twenty years of my life.

I mounted my first Ubar search back in 1968, using two of my platoon's Land Rovers and aiming for the Wadi Mitan. I had with me a quotation from the American archaeologist Dr Wendell Phillips, summarising his failed search: 'The mystery of Ubar remains unsolved. In a completely inaccessible area where today there is little or no camel traffic, a well-marked highway centuries old and made by thousands of camel caravans leads west for many miles from the famous spice lands of Dhofar, and then, on a bearing of N75°W, mysteriously disappears without a trace in the great sands. A dozen Ubars could well be lost among these high dunes, unknown even to the present-day *bedu*. I firmly believe that one day some explorer will solve the mystery of Ubar, Arabia's most intriguing lost city.'

For two days we struggled through the soft sands between Qafa and the Wadi Atinah (see map of Oman p. 25). By the time we reached the then uninhabited site of today's Fasad camp, we had burst two tyres and broken one half-shaft. We travelled on, using the sun and the passage of time, as far due west as the land allowed, and came to a place of a dozen well-trodden camel trails.

On the fourth day we broke our last spare half-shaft and dined with a lone family of Rashidi camel-herders in the dunes. They gave us fresh, frothy camel's milk. We left them water and flour. They knew a man in the Wadi Jadileh, two camel-days west, who would 'have news of Irem'. We made it to the Jadileh but saw nobody in the whole vast, shimmering desert landscape.

From this first failed sortie I learned never to try again without a guide, and to double my stock of spare half-shafts.

We did find Rashidi camel-herders who had lived their entire lives in the area most likely to house Ubar, but none knew of any likely site. For many days we drove into the

dunes and searched high and low until called back to operational work by my sergeant.

Over the next six years I mounted three further attempts to locate Ubar, and all failed, despite many false alarms and raised hopes usually resulting from *bedu* who swore blind they had seen ruins but, when they led us to the spot, professed profound surprise that there was nothing to be seen.

The obvious answer was to search for the city from the air, but throughout the 1980s I kept postponing the project on the grounds that nobody else was searching for Ubar, whereas several rival groups were all keen to be the first to reach the North Pole unsupported.

In the summer of 1990, having recovered from the rigours of a recent, record-setting Soviet journey, I focused anew on Ubar and spent a week in Muscat raising the necessary funds and supplies from old Omani friends. The Sultan of Oman also agreed to help and gave orders to the Royal Oman Police to provide helicopter support as needed, and so I decided to complete a reconnaissance journey immediately, in readiness for a fully fledged archaeological search the following year.

I had agreed with an old film director friend from Los Angeles, Nick Clapp, to run the expedition on a two-prong basis. I would organise the administration and Oman liaison, and lead the expedition in the field, and he would be responsible for filming the entire project. The theme of his film would be the search for Ubar, and he would select a volunteer group of American archaeologists to excavate likely sites as soon as we located them.

Unfortunately for Nick, he and his Los Angeles fundraiser friends were unable to raise any funds and thus stood no chance at all of obtaining Sultanate permission to film in Dhofar. Together, however, we stood a much better chance of achieving our aims.

Following the example of another lost-city searcher, Nick made contact with NASA to request that the Shuttle crew photograph the Ubar search area from space using tele-detection systems to highlight potential sites of the lost city. NASA promised to do their best, and in due course produced a satellite image clearly showing 'well-worn tracks', as well as a nearby L-shaped site that looked man-made. Nick also found a suitable archaeologist, Dr Juris Zarins, with many years of Arabian experience.

We all met up in Dhofar and the reconnaissance got under way, but Juris was singularly unimpressed by the NASA result.

Over the period of our permitted stay in Oman, we had to come up with something new, some rationale to keep our search on the rails. I hotted up the search, using a helicopter to take us to any remote sites where Ubar might conceivably be. Most of these places were the result of stories told to Major Trevor Henry, the Sultan's last remaining British Intelligence officer in Dhofar. Trevor, a tough and enigmatic Scot, had been my sergeant instructor fifteen years before in a long jungle-warfare course in Brunei. He had fought in the Dhofar war, stayed on when peace came, and knew more about the country and its people than any European alive.

Trevor had completed land patrols to, or flights over, all the sites I had queried, whether NASA-identified or *bedu*-rumoured. He had seen nothing of relevance, and told me, 'If the city is out there at all, it has to be sub-surface.' Our whirlwind tour included every known archaeological site in southern Oman that was involved with the frankincense trade.

Juris knew that the reconnaissance had actually proved nothing at all, and he was as surprised as I was when, some months later, the Sultan gave me permission to proceed with the main expedition the following autumn.

We set out in November 1991, and drove three Land Rover Discoveries five hundred miles south from Muscat to Salalah, where I visited the Governor of Dhofar. He gave me permission to excavate any or all of the eleven sites I had listed for him, and also for our team to be based in Shis'r.

From Shis'r our searches over the next two months covered much of Dhofar from the Indian Ocean to the northern sands. In our search for clues we swam underground rivers, descended deep pits and limestone karsts, scraped at burial mounds and frankincense storage vats, wandered numerous desert sites deep in the dunes, and photographed ancient cave paintings. Juris was in seventh heaven, since the whole country was to him an archaeological treasure-house and he was the only archaeologist allowed there by the Sultan.

Such was the power – the wonder – of that dream first sketched out for me by my *bedu* companions.

Nick was also deliriously happy, producing his documentary of a seldom-filmed, remote and fascinating land. Unlike Juris and Nick, I was decidedly unhappy, because this expedition was proving no more successful at lost-city finding than my previous six attempts over the last twenty-three years.

Such was the power – the wonder – of that dream first sketched out for me by my *bedu* companions many years before. I was not going to give up now.

Hi-tech satellite images had not worked, and now traditional searching was faring no better. Although I hate to admit it, our big break, when it came, arrived not through

Above: A member of the Ubar team under a frankincense tree near Kanoon.

Below: One of our Land Rovers disappears in the dunes of Fasad.

deduction or cleverness but through sheer good luck. Or possibly the will of Allah.

Three days before Christmas, shading behind a wall in Shis'r, I was discussing communications problems with Ginny, who was in Dhofar to set up our HF radio systems. In the heat of the midday sun we both fell asleep, and I awoke to hear a heated discussion between two Omanis on the other side of the wall. I recognised their voices. Both were liaison staff from the Ministry of Heritage, whose job was to keep tabs on our activities and report back to their minister. He, in turn, would report to the Sultan.

Their conversation was deeply disturbing. For two weeks they had observed Nick and his team busily filming everything everywhere, although not one archaeological trowel had been raised in earnest. They knew that Juris Zarins and his team of young archaeology students were in Shis'r with all the necessary equipment to hand. So why no digging? It seemed as though archaeology was merely our front, just an excuse to gain coveted permission to make a film of Dhofar generally.

Since the working title for Nick's film was 'The Search for Ubar', it clearly did not really matter much to him whether or not we actually ever located the city. The act of searching was enough to warrant a fascinating film. The two Omanis on whom I had eavesdropped had a good point. I saw big trouble ahead when they made their next report to their minister. There was no time to be lost, so I went straight to Juris. I told him that we were in trouble and he must start digging at once.

'Where?' Juris tilted his Indiana Jones hat back. 'Dhofar is a big place.'

'Anywhere you like,' I begged him. 'Just get digging and make sure the Ministry guys see you at it.'

There was a pile of rubble close by the cliff which jutted over the original waterhole of Shis'r, rubble which a previous French archaeologist acquaintance of Juris had once looked at and logged as mere sixteenth-century remains – useless in terms of Ubar chronology. To dig around existing rubble was a far less pointless exercise than excavating in the middle of nowhere, which was Juris's only alternative.

So, two days before Christmas, with a workforce of just thirteen men, Juris began his methodical attack on the Shis'r rubble in order to allay the suspicions of the local KGB.

After that, everything happened in a rush. Within a week the outline of the rubble heap had taken on the clear-cut silhouette of a ruined tower and a beautifully built horse-shoe structure to its east. Pottery and flints were unearthed hourly, including, to Juris's great pleasure, both Greek- and Roman-style urns from the period that would have been Ubar's heyday.

Days later a piece of red pottery was found which was identical to a unique style found in Uruq, Mesopotamia, altering previous thinking as to the commencement of trade between Mesopotamia and South Arabia from 5000 to 4000 BC. 'This find,' Juris told me, 'could well have a profound effect on many of our evolving theories about the whole history of this area.'

For over five hundred miles of desert in every direction there was no archaeological site with an edifice even a quarter of the size of Shis'r's Ubar. The Ubar towers would have been easily visible from twelve miles away.

Some of the rooms that the team uncovered in our second month at Shis'r yielded rich finds covering the entire period from the second millennium BC until around 300 AD, when trading activities seemed to have dropped off. The finds included six soapstone chess pieces, three inches high,

part of the only chess set ever unearthed in Arabia and well over 1,000 years old. One axe-head was 250,000 years old.

We had found our lost city.

Somehow, we had found our lost city in the exact spot that I had always used as my base camp for twenty-six years . . . from which to look for the lost city.

▲

If I find wonder in the sheer challenge of it all, then the final leg of Transglobe, ten years of work ending with a perilous slog to the North Pole and then onwards to Greenwich, promised to be wonderful indeed.

Given the go-ahead by Sir Vivien Fuchs, Charlie Burton and I came at length to the Bering Straits and our ship ventured into the silted shallows of the mouth of the Yukon river. To the north, her way was blocked by Arctic sea-ice so the plan, made eight years before, was to drop the travel group overboard in rubber boats. We would then go up the Yukon, down the Mackenzie, through the Northwest Passage, and north through the islands of the Canadian archipelago to the most northerly habitation in Canada, our old training base at Alert on Ellesmere Island.

Unless we managed to keep to a rigid rate of progress for over 2,000 hazardous river and sea miles, we would end up frozen in choppy waters sixteen miles off the Yukon. The ship had already 'hit bottom' so she could go no closer to the Alaskan coast. A rogue wave overturned Charlie's heavily laden inflatable and near-disaster ensued. Back on the ship we watched as the skipper edged around wicked shoals until, 200 miles further north, we anchored off the Indian sea

---

village of St Michael. This time our boats made it to the coast, and at length to a tributary of the Yukon, but Charlie's earlier dunking, within view of the *Benji B*, had forced me to rethink my plans for boating the infamous Northwest Passage in the rubber inflatables. The problem was that the loads we each had to carry were just too heavy due to Oliver Shepard's absence (see Chapter 4). I had planned to divide our gear between three, not two, boats. The only solution was to switch to a different type of boat which would cope with our load and the Arctic storms of the Passage. I radioed Ginny, then working as a maid and waitress at the Klondike lodge near Dawson City. This was timely employment as she had no funds, a sponsored Land Rover towing five 45-gallon fuel drums on a trailer, her Jack Russell terrier and, in two weeks' time, the job of transporting us and our boats from a bridge 600 miles up the Yukon to Inuvik on the Mackenzie river.

'We will need a nineteen-foot Boston whaler boat with outboards once we get to Inuvik,' I told her. 'The inflatables will simply not cope with our heavy loads in the big seas of the Passage.'

In between making beds and serving meals, Ginny telephoned desperately around the world to find a boat sponsor. After five days she located a banker in Hong Kong who agreed to buy us a whaler. Frantic work then ensued back in Vancouver, the nearest source of a Boston whaler, and the current berth of the *Benji B*. Two of the ship's crew supervised ice-modifications to the new whaler and Ginny found the boss of a cargo plane who was willing to underwrite its transport to Inuvik. Its arrival there coincided with ours, so no time was lost.

When I had told our boating expert, Anton Bowring, of my plan to switch from the inflatables to an open whaler, he had advised against it.

But I was convinced that a whaler was our only chance now that my inflatables plan had proved ill-conceived by Charlie's near-drowning. There have been many occasions on many expeditions when the experts have counselled against the plan I thought best for the problem ahead. When this happens I try to keep an open mind, always plan for the worst-case scenario, balance all the likely factors against each other, and then go for the best compromise solution. Once the decision is made, I push it hard and fast, and try to forget the ominous warnings of doom from the experts whose advice I have had to ignore.

Once the decision is made, I push it hard and fast.

We said goodbye to Ginny on 26 July. In the thirty-five summer days left, when, with luck, the Passage should remain at least partially ice-free, we had to complete not only the 3,000 miles of the Passage, in which so many ships and men have disappeared, but also cover an additional 500 miles still further to the north in order to be within skiing distance of our Arctic winter quarters before the new ice began to crust over the sea, forcing us to abandon the whaler. Great icebreakers crash through the ice between the islands of the archipelago, but small boats have only navigated the Passage a dozen times, averaging three consecutive summer seasons to do so.

Navigation was a problem. The latest chart was over-printed in large letters: MAGNETIC COMPASS USELESS IN THIS AREA. I visited a Tuktoyaktuk barge captain for advice. 'Don't go,' he said. 'That's the best course for you. My barge has radar beacon responders, MF and DF, and we stay out in

ARCTIC OCEAN

Tuktoyaktuk

Cape Dalhousie

Liverpool Bay

Baillie Island
Snowgoose Passage

Cape Bathurst

Franklin Bay

Booth/Fiji Island

Cape Parry

Clinton Point

BANKS ISLAND

MELVILLE ISLAND

N

Cape Young

VICTORIA ISLAND

Lady Franklin Point

PRINCE OF WALES ISLAND

Cape Storm

Cambridge Bay

Dease Strait

Franklin Strait

Victoria Strait

Pasley Bay

NORTHWEST

TERRITORIES

(CANADA)

Queen Maud Gulf

KING WILLIAM ISLAND

Gladman Point

Gjoa Haven

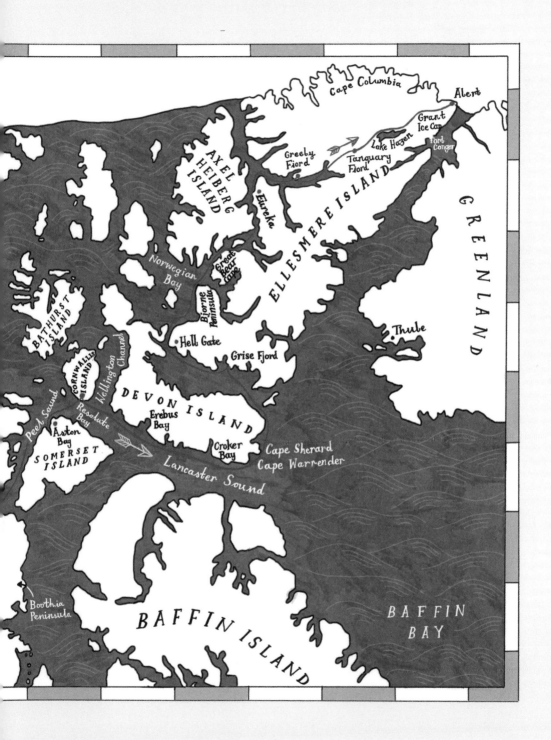

the deep channels. But you must hug the coastline to escape the storms, so you will hit all the shoals. Also, you must stick along the jagged coastline, which looks like the graph of an erratic heartbeat. So you'll have to go much further and will need fuel where there is none. Most of the time it will be thick fog so you'll want to use a compass. But you can't.'

The first month of travel was hectic. If the rolling waves capsized us, as I often thought they would, we would undoubtedly die in the water. Long stretches of coastline offered no landing spot, and the tundra everywhere was uninhabited but for isolated radar sites.

At the next settlement we learned that ice blocked our way east so we detoured south a hundred miles in 30-knot winds and fog. We sheltered from one gale on a tiny island, but on 3 August my patience gave out and we ran through the storm.

We plunged all night between creaming breakers. Twice the whole boat was flung into the darkness as great walls of water struck us broadside.

More by luck than good management, we limped exhausted into the isolated radar station at Gladman Point. The station boss said that we must now wait for the storm to abate as, to the east, the big seas in Victoria Strait would be lethal, and we learned that the local Inuit fishermen had been stranded for five days. 'You must wait,' he advised us. 'The Inuit know best.'

I had no wish to ignore local knowledge, but winter was closing in fast. On 13 August we reached the Passage's half-way point at the Inuit village of Gjoa Haven.

We came to a forty-mile crossing packed with highly mobile ice-floes. Fog descended and a north wind blew the ice towards us. There was no shelter since the coast was lined by sheer cliffs. Rather than risk being crushed in the ice-pack,

To right of centre of this image, our tiny boat threads its way through the floating ice.

I told Charlie that we must turn back and search for the protection of a narrow fjord. He looked most disgruntled, and silence reigned. I was tempted to argue the issue, but I knew this would be a pointless exercise since I was sure that mine was the correct course.

Charlie had often been unhappy when I had progressed despite known risks. The opposite was now true. The whole affair of judging risks can be a touch intuitive and, when time is critical, I will respond to my natural inclination even though others present are strongly advising an alternative course. One key principle I hold dear, a policy much beloved by Field Marshal Montgomery, is never to move against opposition until the cards appear stacked in your favour. Nature can be a tough 'opponent', not given to handing out second chances.

We were pinioned in a fjord for four anxious days, but a wind-change then loosened the ice and we pushed through a labyrinth of floes to Resolute Bay. Again the ice blocked our way north, which was worrying since only six days remained before the sea was likely to freeze over. Pack-ice already seemed to surround us. In a few days we would face a nine-month delay until the following summer, so, taking the bull by the horns, we set out on an unprecedented 900-mile journey with small chance of success.

The founder of the Arctic Institute of North America watched us leave Resolute Bay. He wrote to Andrew Croft: 'Where we were in Resolute, the Fiennes boat came through. They moved off in a snow-storm when the harbour ice had cleared sufficiently – but I tell you that none of us would have changed places with them, sitting high without benefit even of a windscreen.'

Much of the next five days saw us bouncing through rough seas, dwarfed by huge jostling icebergs and sheer black cliffs. For one period of nine hours we saw no landing place and no inlet, however small. Our propeller blades broke, one by one, against unseen chunks of growler-ice and our speed lessened hour by hour.

Charlie spotted a tiny defile, the size of a suburban garden, between two cliffs. In desperation we nosed towards it to change propellers, only to find a polar bear already in residence hunting for beluga whales. Since an unbroken cliff-line stretched east and north for at least the next twenty miles, we nosed in beside the bear and warily changed propellers.

For 120 miles we bucked and rolled between huge icebergs. Some, bigger than bungalows, rolled about like beach balls in the 60-knot gale and freezing sleet.

Back at Resolute, Ginny maintained an unsleeping vigil on her radio, well aware of our vulnerability along these wild, remote coastlines. When I managed to contact her, two days behind schedule, I could hear the tiredness and stress in her voice.

A strong wind kept the new ice from forming in the sea-fjords through the night of 30 August, and by dawn of the new month we saw to our north the dead-end beach of Tanquary Fiord. Snow-capped peaks now blocked our way north. Wolves stared from lava beaches, but nothing moved except us, shattering with our wash the mirror-images of the dark valley walls.

Within four days the boat was frozen into the bay and it was to remain there undisturbed for seven years . . . We had, however, made the first ever open boat journey through the Northwest Passage. With 100-pound loads we skied north over the mountains of Ellesmere Island, switching to snowshoes on steep icy sections. For 150 miles we passed no man-made object, no paths, nothing but rock and ice. In one

Charlie forges on through a frozen valley on Ellesmere Island.

valley our only route lay under a glacier, passing through a blue tunnel carved out by meltwater.

Charlie cut his head open on a rock and deep blisters festered on the soles of both his feet. Our boots broke through the snow's crust into hidden holes, and Charlie jarred his spine. His left eye was swollen shut and his right heel was raw with weeping poison. He no longer wanted to carry his rifle.

'What about bears?' I asked him.

'Good thing,' he muttered. 'They'd put me out of my misery.'

With Charlie's feet and back torturing him, we climbed west of the weird tundra polygons of Black Rock Vale, close by Fort Conger on the coast. In 1924 the American explorer Greely wintered in a hut there. He and his men suffered slow starvation, insanity, cannibalism and death.

The temperature dropped to minus 20°C as, by good luck, we located the hidden entrance to the narrow rock-girt corridor dropping into the upper canyon of the Grant river which falls for thirty miles to the very edge of the continental land mass.

At noon on 26 September we found that the riverbed plunged down a frozen waterfall, and a jagged vista of contorted pack-ice stretched away to the polar horizon that was the Arctic Ocean.

Travelling east along the edge of the semi-frozen sea, we came by dusk to the twin huts of Alert, the most northerly building in the world. We had travelled around the polar axis of the world for 314° degrees of latitude in 750 days. Only 46° more now to Greenwich, but by far the most perilous sector lay ahead.

Within a few days winter arrived at Alert, the temperature plummeted and the sun disappeared. For the next five months Ginny, Charlie and I, with Ginny's dog, lived in the huts at Alert and planned the final phase – the crossing of the Arctic Ocean via the North Pole.

Within yards of our beds, the sea-ice in the bay creaked and groaned in the dark. At times major upheavals and tidal surges cracked the floes apart and the ominous roar of a million tons of ice on the move kept us awake. Soon we would be spending six months trying to traverse 2,000 miles of 'that stuff', as Charlie called it.

No man had ever crossed the Arctic Ocean in a single season, as we had to do. The only crossing in history, four men with forty dogs under Wally Herbert, had taken two summer seasons.

Because we were attempting to go over twice the distance to the Pole prior to the break-up, we needed to set out well before any of our predecessors. Instead of waiting for the comparative comfort of March, with sunlight and warmer temperatures, we had to set out in mid-February in twenty-four-hour darkness and temperatures in the minus 50s.

We left Ginny on 13 February with a wind-chill factor of minus 90°C blowing in our faces. Four days later we found that our way west along the coast was blocked by pressure-ice, so we turned north on to the sea-ice. For days we axed and shovelled a way between ice-walls and boulders for our skidoos and heavy sledges. By 19 February we had slowed to a crawl and I made a snap decision to abandon the skidoos for later collection by ski-plane. We continued immediately, dragging our key stores on man-haul sledges. Our progress through the twilit gloom at once accelerated.

One night back at base, Ginny woke to find our main store hut on fire. She tried to put out the flames, probably ignited by an electrical spark, but with rifle bullets and flares exploding about her, she had to desist, and by morning everything was destroyed.

Although to this point the entire expedition had attracted little media attention, despite its success, our base-camp fire sparked immediate interest all over the world.

On the evening of 7 March, my thirty-eighth birthday, in our tiny tent on the ice we celebrated with two extra cigarettes. That day Charlie's diary recorded: 'We suck ice and snow. There are times when Ran and I have to camp exhausted because we can't pick the axes up. We are shattered. But there is always light at the tunnel's end and that is what you must think about.'

We averaged seven miles of northerly progress each day with the man-haul sledges.

A sudden storm broke up the ice-floes and a sea of dirty sludge moved across the broken edge of our floe. Thick fog then descended. The floes clashed and roared all night.

Back in London a committee report stated: 'At this stage it is fair to say that nobody involved in the expedition would give much for its chances of reaching the Pole this year.'

By now both Charlie and I were suffering from lack of sleep, piles, many areas of raw skin, bloodshot eyes, swollen and bloody fingers, toes, noses and lips, crotch-rot, cracked fillings and a variety of other discomforts. But there was no serious damage, so we began to make good progress as the ice rubble lessened.

We reached the top of the world half an hour before midnight on Easter Day, 10 April. We were the first humans in history to have travelled over the Earth's surface to both Poles, but many hundreds of miles, and cold, wet months, still lay between us and the *Benji B*.

Two weeks after leaving the Pole we reached 86°10' North, having completed some 230 miles of southerly progress, but

The first humans in history to reach both Poles by surface travel.

all around us the sea was opening up. I knew that we must find a safe floe before the break-up began, but Charlie felt that we should concentrate on getting much further south before even looking for safe floes; otherwise, he believed, we would be cut off from any hope of reaching the ship before the ice refroze in four months' time. We discussed our options and I took the safer course of searching for a floe sooner rather than later.

Charlie made his position clear. The decision was mine, not his. The outcome of starting to float too soon from too far north might make us end up well short of the ice-edge and the *Benji B*. If so, all fingers would point at me.

The popular course would be to bash on. But the southerly sea currents were now with us. I used a 1936 Soviet guide, which showed a good mathematical chance that we could float south fast enough to just make it. My natural instinct to hurry on conflicted with an inner instinct to be cautious. The outcome of ten years of work by many people depended on this single decision, and great was our relief when at last we located a solid floe and made camp.

Although there were many scares over the next three months of floating and many new cracks that slowly diminished the floe's size, it took us safely south despite the frequent storms that raged about our fragile home.

Nineteen bears visited the tent over our ninety-five days on the floe. Only one was aggressive, and he was warned off by a bullet through the shin as he attacked.

During the entire duration of our Arctic Ocean journey, Charlie and I had no flare-ups or periods of bad atmosphere. The secret was probably the long period of working together prior to starting the crossing. We were able to recognise each other's stress points so well that we knew almost subconsciously when to steer clear of a delicate topic.

The *Benji B* exits
heavy pack-ice,
pursued by a bear.

On 1 June, Charlie, checking his diary in the tent, muttered, 'By tonight we will have been travelling from Greenwich for 1,000 days.'

Due to strong, southerly winds, our float rate slowed to a crawl and the committee in London worked out that we could not reach any point where we might rendezvous with the ship before that winter. On 2 July the ship tried to force her way towards us, but was driven back. Later that month, eighty-two miles from our floe, the *Benji B* struck ice too hard and a key welding joint in the stern cracked open. Cleverly, the Captain managed to ram another floe in such a way as to run the damaged section high out of the water and, kneeling on the floe, the engineers botched up a temporary repair.

In mid-July the committee, very worried that we would soon be out of reach in the pack-ice, sent orders to Ginny that the ski-plane must try to evacuate us. But Ginny developed 'sudden radio troubles' and failed to receive this evacuation order. At the end of the month, when a wind-change briefly loosened the pack, the *Benji B* tried again.

I think that was the single most satisfactory moment of my life.

On 3 August she became jammed only seventeen miles from our floe. At 2 p.m. that afternoon we abandoned the floe and, using our two portable small canoes on detachable skis, made a dash for the ship on a compass bearing. The canoe skis broke, but we hauled like madmen and, mounting a pressure ridge at 7 p.m., I spotted two tiny matchsticks to the south: the masts of the *Benji B*.

I think that was the single most satisfactory moment of my life.

Wonder: completing the first circumnavigation of
the Earth's polar axis.

For three hours we heaved, tugged, paddled, and often lost sight of the ship, but soon after midnight we climbed on board, back to Ginny and the journey home.

On 24 August Prince Charles brought the ship back to her starting point at Greenwich, almost three years to the day since we had set out. Ten thousand cheering people lined the banks. The journey was over, the circle was complete. Earth had been circumnavigated on her polar axis.

I often think of the sight of that ship. Wonder can be found in the faces of our loved ones, in landscapes or art or religion; or it can be found in the moments when our lives come into crystal focus, the moment when those matchstick masts appear over the horizon and you truly feel you've made a mark. Look out for those moments, and treasure them.

CHAPTER SIX

▲

FAILURE

In order to win at some of your big goals, you are
bound to lose at others along the way.

Ranulph Fiennes

▲

*There is, of course,
no point in crying
over spilt milk.*

──────

In the autumn of 1995, over ten years after the end of Transglobe, I heard that the gossip grapevine in Norway was buzzing. Børge Ousland was planning an attempt to cross Antarctica solo and unsupported in the 1996–97 travel season. Ousland's rationale was clear. All the great polar challenges, north and south, had already been achieved by groups of two or more. All that was left was for an individual to try unaided.

You should never rest on your laurels if you have rivals.

It has always been my belief that you should never rest on your laurels if you have rivals, and my competitive spirit instantly clicked into gear. In truth, solo travel had never appealed to me. Half the fun of an expedition is the planning of it and, as with all old soldiers, the shared memories afterwards. Also, since I make a living through books and talks about the expeditions, I need good photographs and film, which are difficult to get when by myself. On the plus side, however, a lone traveller can experience fewer frustrations caused by rivalry, discontent and, as with Mike and me, differences of pace. Less 'hate' to drive me on, but also a certain freedom.

Ousland was an even better skier than his compatriot Erling Kagge. This was the equivalent of being a footballer even more skilled than Pele. Proof of this was not long in coming when, in the spring of 1996, Ousland reached the

South Pole unsupported in a staggeringly quick forty-four days. Mike and I had taken sixty-eight days to reach the Pole during our 1993 crossing (see the Prologue).

I discussed with Ginny the idea of competing with Ousland to cross Antarctica solo. She shrugged and observed, 'You're not very fit.'

This was true. If I was to enter such a race, I had eleven months in which to train hard, for Ousland would start his solo crossing attempt in October 1996. At thirty-four years of age he was at the peak of his ability. At fifty-two I was getting rusty round the edges, but Mike Stroud had the answer – the Eco-Challenge race. A lot of training and 500 miles later, up against teams from elite special forces units, marathon-runners and orienteering clubs, I successfully dragged myself back to a reasonable level of fitness, but the solo Antarctic crossing attempt which I had long contemplated would need a lot more than physical abilities. I needed a support team, nutritional and medical advice, a communications network and the sort of media coverage that would persuade somebody to sponsor the whole project with at least a quarter of a million pounds.

As always before those journeys that Ginny could not join, she was a tower of strength and sound advice, based on her own wide polar experience. She would check my preparations with meticulous care, and home in on key items I might have forgotten. She was never keen on my leaving her for an expedition, but she never tried to dissuade me from going. This time she was more worried than usual because I was going solo. I felt guilty and selfish and tried to salve my conscience by repeating to myself that, when we married, Ginny had been fully aware of how I intended to make a living.

▲

―――――――

By the time I was ready to attempt the solo crossing of Antarctica, I had spent eleven months becoming what one newspaper described as 'the fittest fifty-two-year-old in Britain, albeit with defective vision, arthritic hips, lower back pain and chronic piles', but I had only spent a few days attempting to master the complex art of kiting, a skill that has a long history in the annals of Polar exploration. One of my sponsors for the expedition, James Dyson, arranged for some training on the Dyson factory's football ground, but this was less than a success. A gust of wind lifted my instructor in the air, he let go, the kite took off for the main road and got run over by a Volvo. Stupidly, I failed to follow up kite work thereafter, which was to prove a costly omission.

Mike Stroud gave me a well-thought-out container of medicaments, tailor-made for the crossing attempt. He also advised me on exactly what rations I should ask Brian Welsby to provide, aiming at 5,600 calories per day as a result of his analysis of our previous expedition work. Mike was now the senior lecturer on nutrition at Southampton University and was the most experienced specialist in survival nutrition in Britain. He also agreed to be spokesman for the expedition, fielding all polar queries from the media.

▲

An American once wrote that 'nothing is more responsible for the good old days than a bad memory', and on my way back to Antarctica, as long-latent memories of gangrene and crotch-rot wormed their way back into my mind, I had to agree with him. Horrid times and subsequent self-promises never to do it again had so often been eclipsed by rose-coloured recollections of journeys past. Now I was at it again. And yet, had I stayed home and watched the news, I would surely have forever regretted letting somebody else grab one of the last remaining polar records without even giving it a go myself.

For a while I had been the only person to cross the continent twice and, on both journeys, had met not a single other human being (apart from at the Pole Station) in a country bigger than China and India joined together. But now there were regular tourist flights to Antarctica, as well as touring cruise ships, with around 15,000 people a year visiting the continent to enjoy the penguin-watching and brave the bracing climate from a position of comfort.

I left at last on the seven-hour flight to Antarctica, three weeks behind my intended start date due to weather problems, and eventually hitched the sledge's dog harness around my chest, shoulders and waist, set my compass for due south and took the strain of my 495-pound load, which included enough fuel and food to last me for 110 days.

A fifty-knot wind from the east slammed at me, blasting my goggles. I could see nothing about me and marvelled at the skill of the recently departed ski-plane pilot. As the sound of the plane ebbed away on the wind, I assessed my position. I didn't have Mike with me, but he had been heavily involved with planning the trip, and I was stocked up with all his pills. Nonetheless, though I wouldn't have admitted it to myself at the time, lurking was the sense of being alone.

I had to stuff such thoughts away smartly. I certainly did not welcome the thought of a solo expedition, but to keep up with the Norwegians, I had to try it. And I still had someone to communicate with, though my radio operator Morag's accent, from the far-flung Orkneys, was challenging to understand at times. Still, at least that would flummox any Norwegians listening in. Somewhere to my right lay the western flank of Berkner Island, perhaps half a mile away.

I must keep clear of its crevasse fields, which had caused Mike and me so much trouble.

After eight hours' stumbling progress the wind-speed shown on my hand anemometer was gusting to eighty knots in the howling polar 'night' and I was falling asleep standing up. Erecting my tiny tent took thirty minutes. Later, on the high polar plateau, I knew this job would have to be done in just three or four minutes, with a wind-chill factor of minus 90°C.

The next day the wind lessened and blew miraculously from the north-north-west, a rare event in that area. So I unfurled my kite and, to my great delight, felt my skis surge forward, hauling me and my 495-pound sledge-load in the approximate direction of the South Pole – until, several times, gusts slammed the sledge into my legs and I collapsed in a welter of skis, sticks and tangled ropes. One high-speed crash gave me a painful ankle and a smashed ski-tip. I bandaged both with industrial tape. This was the learning process.

My heels developed blisters, so I strapped on foam snippets cut from my bed mat and tried to ignore them. My chin, windburnt, became poisoned and swollen, so I lanced it with a scalpel until the swelling subsided. My eyes lost their long-distance focus after a week staring at the glare through goggles. As usual, the lids puffed up with liquid. My eyes became mere slits, and I resembled a rabbit with advanced myxomatosis. Every evening I attended to my developing crotch-rot with Canesten powder and applied lengths of industrial tape to raw areas. My back and hips were sore, but not as painful as on previous journeys because my Dyson harness-designers had developed an effective new padding system. For the first time life was truly bearable, almost enjoyable, on a heavy polar man-haul journey.

One improvement to my man-haul gear of previous years was in the ski-skins department and the superior adhesive mix which glued them to my skis. No longer did they come adrift on uneven ice, so I avoided the frozen fingers caused by repeatedly having to reattach them.

A rare north wind and conditions of good visibility allowed me to once again try my luck at kiting. Without stopping for chocolate, and taking quick gulps of energy orange from my Thermos, I kited 117 miles in one day. I now thought I was almost certain to succeed in the entire crossing. That evening I was only able to eat my day's 5,600-calorie ration by stuffing myself. I did not *need* more than half the ration for I had not exerted myself, merely steered the kite, braced my legs against occasional rough bumps and slid at speed along Berkner Island's rim. So easy. The exact opposite to man-hauling, which would use up 8,000 calories in a typical ten-hour day. That night I unloaded and buried eight full days of rations weighing twenty pounds, due to the extra mileage covered.

To hell with being too old.
It's all in the mind.

I felt elated. To hell with being too old. It's all in the mind. At this stage of our 1993 Antarctic crossing, Mike Stroud and I had already been in a state of semi-starvation and severe physical decline. Yet this time I was still feeling on top form, no more hungry than after a day's training on Exmoor. I was accustomed to the raw skin, poisoned blisters and screaming ligaments which returned on every man-haul trip. The pain in my ankle from the sailing crash was better now, as were the ulcerating blisters on my heels. Life was good, and my competitive urge bubbled up as I set out the next morning, the sledge dragging through the soft new snow.

In a chapter labelled 'Failure', you may have detected signs of hubris in my mood at this point.

▲

On 2 December my Dyson contact told me through whistling static that our charity, Breakthrough's Expedition Appeal, had already raised over £1 million towards the £3 million needed to fund a London breast cancer research centre, and the further I progressed the more money we would raise. I found this a big help when the going was especially hard.

On my twenty-fifth day I was sick a few minutes after eating breakfast gruel. I felt faint and started out four hours behind schedule on a fine sunny day, neither too hot nor too cold. In six hours I man-hauled six miles, despite a long, steep climb. The improved surface continued but I felt queasy and took two Imodium tablets.

Ahead lay only a blue sky and the gently sloping snow-fields leading without further obstruction to the South Pole. I was halfway to the Pole and 125 miles ahead of the point Mike and I had reached in the same time in 1993. I tried not to feel over-optimistic. Things could still go wrong.

To my surprise, I was violently sick again after eating my evening meal, a delicious mixture of ghee milk fat with rehy-drated shepherd's pie and Smash mashed potato.

Two hours later the first cramps attacked my gut and I recognised at once the symptoms of a kidney stone blockage. The pains of a kidney stone, doctors say, are very similar to those of birth contractions – except that they don't produce such a wonderful result. I knew the pain only too well. In 1990 I had had a similar attack on a floating Soviet scientific sea-ice base 200 miles from the North Pole. Another time I had been working in an office, and the stone had been removed surgically within two days. I lit my cooker and heated water.

I would flush the bloody thing out of my system. Drown it with water. Groaning and talking aloud, I wrenched open the medical pack that Mike had meticulously prepared in the knowledge of my 1990 attack, which he had treated.

For twenty-four hours I took more painkillers than the radio doctor had advised and drank a great deal of water, but the stone failed to shift and the pains from my lower stomach, back and sides stayed with me. For an hour or so after each intake of MST, Voltarol and Buscopan the pain was muted and my desire to continue the journey mounted. Then the dreaded spasms returned with ever-increasing intensity, and I writhed about on the cold floor of the tent clasping my flanks and rolling into a foetal ball incapable of constructive thought processes.

On 27 December, with two days of tablets left, I decided that the danger of irreparable damage to my kidneys, as well as the risk of running out of painkillers, was too great a price to pay for the chance of being first to cross the Antarctic solo. I pulled the pin of my emergency beacon, which a few hours later informed a satellite signal watcher in England who, in turn, alerted the Twin Otter ski-plane crew at Patriot Hills as to my exact position.

Nine hours later, with the fine weather beginning to change, the Twin Otter landed by my tent. Throughout the flight back to Patriot Hills, the Australian doctor fed morphine into my blood system through a drip. I was soon completely stoned and in wonderful, painless bliss. My journey had ended almost exactly halfway to the South Pole and a quarter of the way to my destination on the far side of the continent.

Assessing the whole enterprise afterwards, my big mistake, I realised, had been to concentrate during training on man-haul fitness rather than on becoming a wind-assistance expert. Using wind assistance with kites or para-wings is very different from using following-wind devices such as parachutes or dinghy sails which were employed by Amundsen, Shackleton and Scott. The toil and the suffering is cut to a minimum and that, after all, is what leads to success.

Back at home a month later, James Dyson called to say that the Breakthrough fundraisers had already raised £1.7 million and that he would personally add £700,000 to that total. He had produced a new 'polar-blue' Dyson model that month, and £10 from the sale of each unit was added to our fund. At the time, one in every twelve British women was being hit by breast cancer. The money raised by the expedition, even though it failed to achieve its physical goal, allowed Breakthrough to help set up Europe's first dedicated breast cancer research centre. The solo expedition had failed as a physical challenge but, thanks to James, not as a charity project.

▲

I had failed in Antarctica, but Ginny was, as always, a sympathetic shoulder to lean on. We went skiing in Courchevel, the activity and the place that we both loved best. We made plans to spend much more time together, although I had learned at least twenty years before never to promise Ginny that I would do no more expeditions.

As it turned out, early in 1999, a publisher offered me an excellent contract to try again to reach the North Pole solo and unassisted and taking plenty of camera 'selfies' en route. Ginny agreed that other income sources were not looking good at the time, and I had been keeping pretty fit. Age-wise, I suspected that this would be my last polar record attempt and I was not exactly lacking in the relevant skills. I would also expect to raise £2 or £3 million for a chosen charity.

Lady Luck and poor judgement on my part cut this venture short when, less than a few miles from my departure point on Ward Hunt Island, a surge by a thin ice-floe occurred without warning and a slab tilted suddenly under the sledge, which responded to gravity and, unbalancing me, pulled me backwards. I fell on my back and slid down the slab. The noise that followed was the one I most hate to hear in the Arctic – a splash as the sledge fell into the sea.

The noise that followed was the one I most hate to hear in the Arctic – a splash as the sledge fell into the sea.

I kicked out with my skis and flailed at the slab with both hands. One ski boot plunged into the sea and one gloved hand found an edge of the slab. Taking a firm grip, I pulled my wet foot and ski out of the water. I unfastened the man-haul harness. I was already beginning to shiver. I squirmed around until I could sit on a flatter slab to inspect the sledge in the gloom. It was underwater, but afloat. I hauled on the traces, but they were jammed under the slabs. Seventy days' worth of food and thirty of fuel were on that sledge – and the communications gear. Without it, the expedition was over. A nearby slab crashed into the sea: the ice was moving. I had to save the sledge quickly. Soon I would be dangerously cold.

With my feet hooked around a slab, I lay on my stomach and stretched my left arm under the slab to free the sledge trace. I took off my mitt so that I could feel where the rope was snagged. For a minute or so I could not find the underwater snag. Then, by jiggling the rope sharply, it came free. I pulled hard and the sodden sledge rose to the surface. My wet hand was numb but I could not replace the mitt until the sledge was out of the sea. Gradually the prow rose on to

---

a slab and water cascaded off its canvas cover. Minutes later the sledge was on 'dry land'. I danced about like a madman. Both my mitts were back on and I used well-tried cold-hands revival techniques to restore life to the numb fingers. Usually they work and my blood returns painfully to all my fingers; this time they did not.

I had seen enough frostbite in others to realise that I was in serious trouble.

I took the wet mitt off and felt the dead hand. The fingers were ramrod stiff and ivory white. They might as well have been wooden. I knew that if I let my good hand go even partially numb, I would be unable to erect the tent and start the cooker – which I needed to do quickly for I was shivering in my thin man-haul gear. The next thirty minutes were a nightmare. The cover zip jammed. With only five useable but increasingly numb fingers, precious minutes went by before the zip was freed and I unpacked the tent. By the time I had eased one tent-pole into its sleeve, my teeth were chattering violently and my good hand was numb. I had to get the cooker going in minutes or it would be too late. I crawled into the partially erect tent, closed its doorzip and began a twenty-minute battle to start the cooker. I could not use the petrol lighter with my fingers, but I found the matches I always carried with a striker in a screw-lid tin.

Starting an extremely cold petrol cooker involves careful priming so that just the right amount of fuel seeps into the pad below the fuel jet. The cold makes washers brittle and the priming plunger sticky. Using my teeth and a numb index finger, I finally worked the pump enough to squirt fuel on to the pad, but I was slow in shutting off the valve, and when

---

I applied the match a three-foot flame reached to the roof. Luckily I had had a custom-made flame lining installed, so the tent was undamaged. And the cooker was alight – one of the best moments of my life.

Slowly and painfully some feeling came back into the fingers of my right hand. An hour later with my body warm again, I unlaced my wet boot. Only two toes had been affected. Soon they would exhibit big blood blisters and lose their nails, but they had escaped true frostbite. All around the tent cracking noises sounded above the steady roar of the cooker. I was in no doubt as to the fate of my bad hand. I had seen enough frostbite in others to realise that I was in serious trouble. I had to get quickly to a hospital to save some fingers from the surgeon's knife. I had to turn back.

I hated the thought of leaving the warmth of the tent, and both hands were excruciatingly painful. I set out in great trepidation. Twice my earlier tracks had been cut by newly open leads, but fortunately it needed only small diversions to detour the open water. Five hours later I was back on the ice-shelf. I erected the tent properly and spent three hours massaging my good hand and wet foot over the cooker.

When at length I made it back to the hut on Ward Hunt Island I erected the tent on the floor, clumsily started the cooker and prepared the communications gear. I then spoke to Resolute Bay who promised to evacuate me the following day on the Twin Otter scheduled flight due to change over the weathermen at Eureka.

The fingers on my left hand began to grow great liquid blisters. The pain was so bad that I raided my medical stores for drugs. The next day I found an airstrip near the hut and marked its ends in the moonlight with kerosene rags. When I heard the approaching ski-plane I lit the rags and prayed the First Air pilot would not funk the landing. He didn't, and some forty-eight hours after my arrival at the hut I was on my way to try to save my left hand.

The following night I flew to Iqaluit on Baffin Island where, after intravenous antibiotic therapy, a doctor started to open up the big finger blisters. After transference to the Ottawa Hospital, I was in the hands of frostbite experts Doctors Conrad Watters and Heather O'Brien. Their initial report stated: 'The left hand demonstrates severe thermal injury to all five digits. The thumb is blistered from the mid portion and the fingers are all oedematous throughout the course. His right foot is remarkable for areas of frostbite covering a coin-sized area of the distal great toe and a corresponding portion of the second toe on the right side. He was unaware of this injury prior to changing his clothing to begin hyperbaric treatment. I am optimistic that he can get some benefit from aggressive and immediate hyperbaric oxygen therapy.'

I called Ginny, whose immediate reaction to my being less able to help with the cattle was, 'Typical, and we're already short-handed on the farm.' To a *Times* reporter she commented, 'We know several people here on Exmoor who have lost bits of fingers, or worse, in farm machinery or as a result of ferret bites. As long as Ran doesn't leave his finger bits on the edge of the bath, as he once did with a blackened toe, I'll be happy to see him back next week. He did put on a lot of extra weight for the expedition, so now he'll have to take it off again. I might hide the farm machinery and give him a dung fork to clear the cowshed by hand.'

I returned to Britain with another failure under my belt, a scant amount raised for our charity and a disappointed sponsor. Kidney stones and frostbitten digits are no more acceptable to critics as reasons for failure than are unseasonal polar storms or crevasse accidents. I suppose that, over a twenty-six-year period of polar travel, the frostbite odds were always narrowing, and this time they had caught up with me, which was a shame because everything was otherwise looking good, the sledge was going well, and I was in peak condition.

There is, of course, no point in crying over spilt milk since, if you go for the big ones and you win some in your lifetime, you can be sure you will lose at others on the way. The best course, I've usually found, has been to shrug, note what you have done wrong and apply yourself quickly to trying again.

This, my standard policy over the years, did not look like it was working this time because my damaged fingers were liable to be subject to further amputation shortly, which would seriously affect extreme-cold projects in the future. One of my firm rules in selecting individuals for polar travel had always been to avoid anyone, however experienced or skilled, who had any history of frostbite damage. Badly bitten noses and ears were okay. Fingers and toes were not.

I also knew that this Arctic failure, coming hot on the heels of the Antarctic solo kidney stone, was asking for trouble from the UK media who are almost as eager to savage a failed expedition leader as a football manager who has lost a couple of key matches. Most of them enjoyed being witty at my expense. *The Times* offered me solid advice: 'It is a reasonable bet that if Sir Ranulph's frostbitten hand allows it, he will be planning to trudge through the snow again. Doggedness and fortitude saved his life on this occasion, but he was fortunate to survive and time is not on his side. The older someone is, the more they are liable to suffer from hypothermia, frostbite and diseases associated with the cold. The reflexes that come into play to protect skin when its temperature is dangerously lowered are less efficient, so corrections to skin temperature may be slow and frostbite more likely. So Sir Ranulph should opt for holidays in Spain.'

▲

*Shrug, note what you have
done wrong and apply yourself
quickly to trying again.*

———

Media barbs the week after I returned home from Ottawa were easily kept in perspective by the more immediate worry of what to do about my damaged fingers. They throbbed most of the time and complained loudly with needle-sharp pain when brought into contact, however lightly, with any object, even clothing material. To avoid this, especially when trying to sleep, was often difficult. Two of my friends who were surgeons advised speedy amputation of the damaged finger to avoid complications such as gangrene. After checking the records of a number of specialists, Ginny found a surgeon in Bristol, Donald Sammut, with a history of brilliant treatment of damaged fingers. The south-west of England produces very few frostbite cases, but so what? Damaged fingers are all the same once cut off, whatever the original reason for the trauma, and I was greatly relieved when Donald agreed to deal with my fingers.

A friend from the Institute of Naval Medicine in Portsmouth, for whom I had previously completed cold-water research work in his immersion tank, telephoned out of the blue. Under no circumstances, he warned, should I undergo any amputations until at least five months after the date of the accident.

'Why not?' I asked, perplexed.

The Navy surgeon explained that he had seen many divers with toe and finger damage which had been operated on too early before the semi-traumatised tissue that lies between the dead ends and the undamaged stumps had had time to heal properly.

'This is the tissue,' he stressed, 'that will be needed – after the dead finger ends are cut away – to stretch over the stumps. So it must be strong, elastic, healthy tissue; not severely damaged, as it is now. More fingers have been shortened unnecessarily by premature surgery than by the original damage from the bends or from frostbite. So don't you let them cut you up too early, Ran, or you'll regret it. Your new stump material will simply fail to do its job and you'll end up back on the chopping block with even shorter fingers.'

But after four months of living with grotesque, witch-like talons, purple in colour, sticking out of my stumps, I could take it no longer and, with another month to go before Donald Sammut was due to cut them off, I decided to take the matter into my own hands. Each and every time over the previous sixteen weeks that my fingers had hit or merely brushed against anything, never mind something hot, I had sworn at the pain. Ginny suggested that I was becoming irritable.

The answer was obvious. The useless finger ends must be cut off at once, so they could no longer get in the way and hit things. I tried tentatively to cut through the smallest finger with a new pair of secateurs, but it hurt. So I purchased a set of fretsaw blades at the village shop, put the little finger in my Black & Decker folding table's vice and gently sawed through the dead skin and bone just above the live skin line. The moment I felt pain or spotted blood, I moved the saw further into the dead zone. I also turned the finger around several times to cut it from different sides, like sawing a log. This worked well and the little finger's end-knuckle finally dropped off after some two hours of work. Over that week I removed the other three longer fingers, one each day, and finally the thumb, which took two days.

My physiotherapist congratulated me on a fine job, but Donald Sammut was not so happy. I apologised to Donald, but felt secretly pleased with myself since life improved considerably once the gnarled and mummified ends no longer got in the way. Ginny agreed that I had done the right thing.

After all, she no longer had to tie my tie for me, nor put in my cufflinks before I gave a conference talk.

▲

I'm certainly not one of life's Pollyannas. My second wife, Louise, tells me to stop whingeing quite a lot. And whereas on expeditions the next step is usually obvious, in real life it can be hard to see the path forwards. Such is the temptation of 'an easy way out' that you see in the news all the time, affecting rich and poor alike.

But if I catch myself being gloomy, I *do* draw on my experiences at the ends of the Earth. Clearly, the story of my frostbitten hands shows an extreme solution to an extreme event. But it is emblematic of how I have always approached the slings and arrows of life, and I hope that there is a nubbin of wisdom there for anyone facing failure. As in the famous quote attributed to Confucius, our greatest glory is not in never falling, but in rising every time we fall. Whatever life throws at you, you have a choice. I could have reacted to the injury to my hand by hanging up my gloves and seeking a quieter life, but instead I chose the opposite: to double down. As you will see in the next chapter, there was no doubt that I would carry on, and if it proved impossible, fair enough. But not without trying. If polar travel now looked difficult, then I would simply have to move on to mountains instead.

If I have no fingers, then I must learn to climb without fingers. What happened to them is not in my power; my reaction to the event is.

CHAPTER SEVEN

▲

FACING FEAR

It is easier to avoid fear than to overcome it.

Ranulph Fiennes

▲

*The key is to have the courage
to share your fears with someone
you trust, to ask for help
and accept it.*

———

When we reached the spot, my mouth was bone dry and my hands like jelly. This was the key moment of the whole climb and I attacked it in a rush, desperate to keep my mind busy with no tiny chink into which sheer terror could claw and render me an embarrassment to myself and to the others. The fear of the mountain fought the fear of my own ego as I tried to concentrate on finding the next tiny crack in the glistening rock in which to place the steel points on my crampons. I gripped the black rope where I had watched my guide Kenton hold it, and edged down around the bulge – and into space. Suddenly, and with a surge that took my breath away, there was a yawning panoramic view of the world below. For almost half a mile under my boots, only the wind touched the plunging rock of the fearsome Eiger. My crampons scrabbled desperately to find a hold. Into my brain, unbidden, came the picture of my heavy body tearing Kenton off the cliff, and then the deadweight of us both pulling our companion Ian away, and the rush of air as we cartwheeled through space . . .

▲

We all face fears in our daily lives. The fear of failure or rejection; the fear of losing those we love; the fear of pain. I have always suffered from two strong fears throughout my life: of heights, and spiders. As a boy growing up in South Africa, I remember a spider jumping out of my mother's curtains and biting me on the back of the neck before school one morning. When we left South Africa to move to England when I was eleven or twelve, I found that even the stupid little English spiders scared me, and it wasn't until I went to join the Arab army in Oman that I was forced to really face my fears.

When the little plane dropped me off in Oman and I turned to meet the thirty men who would be under my leadership for the next two years, all staring at this young Brit who had just appeared in the middle of the desert. On that first evening they had got a fire going, goat meat roasting away and thirty pairs of eyes watching me as I ate – and a bloody great eight-inch wolf spider covered in eyes and hairy legs came across the top of my trouser leg. I know I would ordinarily have sworn out loud and smashed it, but the fear of losing respect in front of my new charges was so great that I sort of grinned at this thing . . . and it didn't bite. For two years those spiders came in and out of my sleeping bag, and eventually, through forced habitation, I managed to control my fear.

As for heights, bear in mind that even at school I was only able to climb buildings at night because that way I couldn't see the drop, and this tactic even saw me through the SAS. Our jump instructor was adamant that I must keep my eyes open when jumping out of a plane; so of course, being naughty, I kept them closed. I have never been afraid of strenuous physical effort, of pushing my body to its absolute limits through difficult conditions. But I have always retained my irrational fear of heights (or rather drops).

I write later in this book about my battles against Everest, but if I was to attack my phobia of heights, the daddy of all nasties lies a mere three-hour drive from Geneva Airport: the North Face of the Eiger, the notorious Nordwand, the North Wall.

Having trained with my expert guide Kenton Cool (see Chapter 3) and developed strategies for climbing with my in-jured hand, on 1 March 2007 I flew to Geneva with my family and drove a rental car to Grindelwald, where we stayed at a

small hotel, the Grand Regina, with a reputation among British tourists for being the best in all Switzerland. The hotel manager, Ingo Schmoll, warned us of the consequences of the mountains not being as stable as they should normally be in mid-winter. The rate of retreat of glaciers throughout the Alps, together with the thawing of the permafrost layer, had created temporary barrages of fallen rock blocking high ravines and creating lakes. Increasingly torrential summer rains then burst the feeble dams of rubble, causing flash floods, mudslides and more loosened rock. The previous autumn the Eiger itself had suffered a major rockfall, a chunk bigger than two Empire State Buildings.

Kenton, in Chamonix, was in touch with Ralph Rickli, the famous Swiss Met forecaster in Berne, and with the top European weather bureau, the Met Office in Exeter. We needed a clear good-weather window of at least five days and nights on the North Face if a non-skilled climber like me was to reach the summit.

I began to find the bulk of the Eiger, looming over the hotel, a touch oppressive. This is a key point about fear in general: so much of it is in the idea of the thing you are afraid of, the anticipation. I tried to keep busy. I went for a daily two-hour run out of the village, along hilly lanes and up the glacial ravines. As I ran, I heard the intermittent explosions of avalanches from the heights of the Alpine giants all around. After six days of evil weather forecasts, I was padding about Grindelwald increasingly worried that we would never get a five-day clear period in March. Every time I looked out of the window or trudged through the village streets, I found myself looking up at that great black wall, the upper limits obscured in thick fog. One night I couldn't sleep and spotted a single pinprick of light high up on the bulk of the North Face. The very sight of it made my stomach muscles tighten

▲

*So much of fear is in the idea
of the thing you are afraid of,
the anticipation.*

———

as I imagined having to try to sleep anywhere on that hideous cliff.

I went for a walk to a mountain coffee house and paid £3 in Swiss francs for a 'Rockslide' (a coffee spiked with schnapps) named in honour of the recent big Eiger rockfall. I sat there for three hours and frightened myself reading of Joe Simpson's Eiger experience in 2002. At last our friendly weather experts in Berne and in Exeter concurred, and a five-day window was forecast for the middle of the month.

When Kenton finally confirmed our imminent departure, I tried to hide the fear, almost panic, that surged with the knowledge that we were about to start the climb. Until then there was always the doubt about the weather, the chance that we might not be able to try the climb at least until the following September. But now the die was cast. Later that day, in the hostel at the foot of the Eiger, I needed to work hard to appear unfazed in the boisterous company of Kenton, Ian Parnell, the ITV crew and Stephen Venables, who was reporting on the climb for *The Sunday Times*.

We were to leave the hostel for the hour-long snow traverse to the base of the North Face at 4 a.m. the next morning and I found sleep elusive that night. I remembered a hundred similar sleepless nights before big moments, but polar fears were something I knew how to handle. Mountain fears were different. I feared my own inadequacies, of being revealed as a coward or, at best, a wimp. Would the North Face trigger uncontrollable vertigo? Would I freeze to some cliff, unable to move, thereby risking Ian's and Kenton's lives, as well as my own? Never mind the ridicule. And what of a fall? I had by now read all the accounts by far better climbers than myself.

But I had learned the secret of dealing with fear in Dhofar, faced with the daily terror of some bullet, shrapnel shard

Thinking about anything but the jump onto the Fabergstolsbre glacier in Norway.

or mine blast ripping out my genitals or blinding me. I had learned the secret all over again some years later, training for a dizzying parachute jump onto the Fabergstolsbre glacier in Norway, letting go of the wing strut of our little Cessna seaplane and needing to jump sideways and outwards in order to avoid decapitation: Keep a ruthlessly tight clamp on your imagination. With fear, you must prevent, not cure. Fear must not be let in in the first place. Think of anything but the subject of your fear. Never look at the void you are about to jump into. If you hear a bird flying below your feet or the church bells chiming in the valley below, don't think of the bird, don't listen to the bells. If you are in a canoe, never listen to the roar of the rapid before you let go of the river-bank. Just do it! Keep your eyes closed and let go. If the fear then rushes at you, it will not be able to get a grip, because your mind will by then be focusing on the technical matter of survival as the mechanics take over. As long as you are concentrating on how you're going to get that hand, with no finger ends, into that hold above you, you will have no room for fear to get a look in.

Keep a ruthlessly tight clamp on your imagination. With fear, you must prevent, not cure.

▲

Such tactics are all very well when coping with rational fears about what *might* happen. But vertigo is not rational and the trigger likely to set it off was the all too real sight beneath my feet of a great beckoning, sickening void. Exactly what would it feel like to spend time cartwheeling, rushing downwards for several thousand feet?

Once my alarm went off and I began to check all my gear before a rushed breakfast, the dread thoughts and fears of the night did indeed disperse. We left on time in pitch darkness with Kenton leading.

I thought of its German nickname: *Mordwand*, or Murder Wall.

Ian's backpack was heavier than mine due to all the camera gear, as he was to document the climb and attempt a series of live ITV News broadcasts. Kenton's pack, also heavier than mine, was festooned with climbing paraphernalia, but I still felt dubious about climbing with a pack that restricted my movement, cramped my arms and limited my ability to look upwards. Dawn crept over the Alps and the mountain tops were tipped with an orange alpenglow. The stars disappeared and the great wall above us came alive. I thought of its German nickname: *Mordwand*, or Murder Wall.

Half an hour of trudging along a line of boot prints in deep snow took us to the spot Kenton decided to climb from.

We fixed on our crampons beneath a feature known as the First Pillar. Many climbers lose the route in this area, but Kenton seemed confident as he stared up at our first obstacle, some 2,000 feet of mixed snow gullies, loose scree, shiny ledges of smooth, compact limestone and temporarily lodged boulders.

Few of the infamous Eiger tragedies occurred on this first 2,000-foot climb, but the fallen detritus of many an Eiger incident lay all around us. I remember, from one of the Eiger books, a photograph of climber Edi Rainer's body lying smashed in the scree of this catchment zone. And Chris Bonington, on his Eiger ascent, had among these rubble-strewn lower reaches passed by blood trails and a piece of flesh attached to some bone.

I knew that the world's top soloists, acrobats of the top league, could climb the *Mordwand* in hours, not days, without ropes, in their sticky-soled rock-shoes, as light as woollen socks. A single slip or false move would see them dead, crushed on the rock, but they survive on the confidence born of their expertise. The mere thought of climbing a single rock pitch unroped made me flinch.

We must have climbed some 2,000 feet up the mountain when we reached the next recognisable feature, the aptly named Shattered Pillar. I was feeling tired and my neck muscles were aching from the tug of my rucksack harness. But the weather was, as prophesied by the Met Offices of Berne and Exeter, holding good and clear. Every few hours I tore open a new hand-warmer bag with my teeth and inserted the two tiny pouches into my mitts. They worked well, and whenever the sensitive stumps of my amputated fingers began to feel numb with cold, I positioned the hand-warmer pouch over their ends for a while.

I had never climbed on similar rock before, smooth like slate with almost nowhere to provide even the tiniest holding point for the tips of my ice-axes and crampon spikes. At times I had to remove one or other of my mitts with my teeth and use my bare hand to clasp some rock bulge or slight surface imperfection to avoid a fall. This I hated to do, for my fingers, once cold, took forever to re-warm, even with my heat pouches.

Every now and again I glanced below me without thinking and felt that shock of terror I knew so well which presages the first wave of vertigo. I instantly forced my mind to concentrate on something of interest above me, usually Kenton's progress. On that first day this process worked well for me. I was, due to vanity, keen to prevent Ian and Kenton from glimpsing my fear.

At some point on a steep icy slope, to my considerable alarm and dismay, one of my boots skidded off a nub of protruding rock and my left crampon swung away from my boot. Although still attached by a strap, the crampon was useless. Luckily the same crampon had come loose once before, on a frozen waterfall with Kenton a month ago. So I reined in my rising panic and, hanging from one axe and a tiny foothold, I managed, with much silent swearing, to reattach the crampon to the boot.

Don't look down. Don't think down.

We came, over 2,000 feet up, to an eighty-foot-high rock face known as the Difficult Crack, which I found virtually impossible, far more technically demanding than any of my previous training ascents, and extremely testing on my puny biceps. To be more precise, my arms felt as though they were being torn from their sockets since, in the almost total absence of any reasonable footholds, I had literally to haul my body and rucksack upwards by arm-power alone. I wished I had spent more time obeying Kenton's instructions to train hard at obtaining some upper body strength. By the time I heaved myself up the last steep and glass-smooth boulder of the Crack, I was on my very last ounce of willpower and wanted only to stop for the day and sleep. Not that there was anywhere remotely suitable in sight to lie down or even to sit.

Ian recorded my ascent of the Difficult Crack: 'Through Ran's two years of training for the route, he proved himself to be a competent and efficient ice and mixed climber, but steep rock tended to bring out his weaknesses. In particular, his ineffectual stumps for fingers on his left hand . . . Ran's worst fear was that he might be forced to climb bare-handed. Luckily he had one big advantage. Whereas Kenton and I spent valuable time fretting and testing the security of the meagre hooks we'd uncovered, Ran, to put it bluntly, was clueless. His technique basically involved dragging his tools down the rock until they somehow snagged, then he would blindly pull for glory. His footwork on rock was similarly polished: a wild pedalling technique that for all its dry tooling naivety was surprisingly effective.'

From the top of the Difficult Crack we could look immediately above us at an immense sheer wall, known as the Rote Fluh, smooth, red and infamous for its propensity to shower loose rockfalls on to the face below.

From the Crack we still had more than 8,000 feet of climbing, including traverses, on the North Face, much of which, I knew, would be a lot harder and more exposed than had been the eighty-foot-high Crack.

Kenton had planned for us to bivouac the first night at a ledge known as the Swallow's Nest. Between Difficult Crack and this refuge was the infamous Hinterstoisser Traverse, unlocking access to the centre of the wall. It was a key passage won at considerable cost by its pioneers, two German guides, Andreas Hinterstoisser and Toni Kurz, and two Austrian guides, Willy Angerer and Edi Rainer.

Their story forms a part of the forbidding history of this section of the face. In 1935 a couple of Germans, Sedlmayer and Mehringer, had climbed a record distance up the mountain, but at 3,300 metres they had frozen to death on a ledge. A year later Hinterstoisser and his companions, hoping to set a new record, if not to get to the summit, had reached the ledge of the frozen bodies which, with climbers' macabre humour, they named Death Bivouac, only to be themselves turned back by the weather and falling rocks. But fatally they had left no rope in place across their key traverse, and their desperate attempts to reverse their route over this slippery, vertical cliffside all failed. One fell and dropped free to the valley below, one was strangled by the rope, and a third froze to death.

I recall, at some point during that fearful move, noticing a sudden whiteness in the black rope, the rope upon which I was utterly dependent each time my crampons slipped away from the face. Somehow the rope had become frayed at this point to a single fragile strand.

Somehow the rope had become frayed at this point to a single fragile strand.

When I eventually came to the far side of the traverse, Ian recorded: 'Ran emerged near the end looking by his standards pretty nervous – not one to shout his complaints, his eyes were wide open and out on stalks which betrayed what he was really thinking . . . So, when he started slipping down, his cramponed feet pedalling for purchase on blank rocks, sparks flying, I think he felt desperate measures were needed. The nearest thing at hand to assist him was his ice-axe, so he took an almighty lunge up at the ropes and pulled himself to safety. The only problem was that his "safety" was reliant on the one-centimetre-thick cord of nylon he had snapped with his razor-sharp axe blade and which secured *me* to the belay.'

I clambered past Ian's body and savoured the blessed relief of a solid six-inch ledge under one crampon. I rested on it and felt a wave of exhaustion pass through me. So had I conquered my fear of heights? Had I vanquished my sixty-two-year-old bogeyman of vertigo? I *had* crossed the Hinterstoisser Traverse on the great North Face of the Eiger, so surely I *must* have become a 'proper climber'. And proper climbers surely don't fear heights. Yet I suspected that nothing had really changed. There had been no actual confrontation within myself. No fearful struggle that I had bravely and finally won. My only victory thus far had been to prevent the creeping angst getting a grip on me. Day One on the Eiger was almost over without a disaster. Three or four more days, ever higher, lay ahead.

From the end of the traverse, we inched up a seventy-foot vertical crack to an eighteen-inch-wide ledge beneath an overhang, the Swallow's Nest. A scab of frozen snow was stuck to the ledge and we used our axes to flatten this out, giving us some four feet of width and almost standing-up space. Ian clipped my waist harness to a rock bolt, and Kenton melted snow over a tiny gas stove. Our bivouac was comfortable but, for me, ruined by the knowledge that, as I lay with my nose up against the rock wall and my knees curled up for warmth in the lightweight sleeping bag, my backside protruded over the edge of our ledge and over the void below.

▲

During the night a breeze blew ice-dust down the neck of my jacket and small stones clattered by. I resisted the temptation to roll over and sleep facing outwards. The clear night sky was crammed with stars, mirrored by the pinprick lights of Grindelwald in the dark valley below. Kenton woke us before dawn. He passed me an empty cloth bag which I filled with snow blocks that I cut, reluctantly, from the end of my sleeping platform. Ian asked me for some item and, unthinkingly,

I threw it along the ledge to him, forgetting for an instant where we were. This deserved and got a mouthful of abuse from the others. '*Never*,' they cried in unison, 'throw anything. Pass it over with care.' Ian went on to warn me about my boots and crampons. 'Put them on carefully. It's all too easy with cold hands trying to force a cold foot into a rigid boot to lose your grip and then, before you know it, a boot is gone – a long way. Then you are in *serious* trouble.'

Answering the call of nature during the first day's climb was something I had successfully postponed, but the moment of truth arrived on the narrow ledge. There was a sharp breeze and I felt cold. Squatting between the rock face and the void, I was thankful for the small mercy that I was up one end of the ledge and not, like Ian, in the middle. Luckily I had an empty polythene bag to hand as a receptacle. Nonetheless, I did begin to wonder how climbers cope on big mountain faces having to drink water from the soiled snow floors of oft-used ledges.

Shortly before sunrise, Kenton disappeared upwards from the Swallow's Nest. Soon after I followed his lead onto the ice-slope above our bivouac, there came an awkward lean-ing move over the face of a smooth rock. For a while I was flummoxed, but, stretching the axe in my good hand fully upwards, I felt its spike lodge in some unseen nook. Such moments require a blind hope that your sole hold on life will be a reliable one when you make the next move. If it isn't and your sudden bodyweight dislodges the axe's placement, you will plummet downward, hoping not to drag your colleagues with you.

Once over the rock I was on to a long steep icy slope known as the First Ice-Field, and here I heard the whistling thrum of solid matter falling past us, whether ice or rock I was not sure. The day before, a small stone had struck Kenton's helmet, and at the base of this First Ice-Field, arrowing up-wards at some 55 degrees, a largish lump of ice caught Ian on the helmet.

With careful axe work, I crawled up two steep slopes of mixed rock and ice with extreme caution, for there was a deal of loose rubble just itching to respond to the call of Isaac Newton. After 200 feet negotiating this unstable zone, we scaled the first real ice-field, which I found less difficult than anything to date. It ended all too quickly at the bottom end of a 300-foot-high near-vertical gully of part-iced rock known as the Ice Hose. I definitely disliked this section which, as an amateur, I find difficult to describe. I saw simply a forbid-dingly smooth expanse of rock, pebble-dashed here and there by ice, snow and rubble.

More stones whistled by as I inched up the Hose but, although I found myself flinching and ducking, none made contact, and the next time I reached Kenton's belay position, he looked happy, clearly pleased that we had reached the Second Ice-Field intact. This was the great white sheet easily identifiable from Grindelwald. At some point as we axed our way up it, Kenton saw an ice-axe whistle by us on its way down the face. We never did identify its owner. I shiv-ered at the thought of trying to climb any distance at all on such a mountain with only one axe. The wind picked up on the wide-open flank of the ice-field. An explosion sounding further down the face, as we learned later from Philip and his ITV film crew, came from an avalanche of rock and ice roaring down the Ice Hose that we had earlier scaled. The ice-climb seemed to go on and on, and our ropes were usually slack between each other, to the extent that I felt as though I was almost free-climbing un-roped. On the many soft snow patches, I took special care to dig in my spikes and axes as deeply as I could.

Kenton, seeing that I was flagging badly on a difficult section, had pointed upwards. 'Only two or three pitches to Death Bivouac,' he assured me. The name of the place was hardly reassuring. Just then, however, Kenton's promise of its proximity did make it sound a very welcome spot. Again we dug away at a snow-clogged ledge and cleared enough space for the three of us to lie head to toe. The legendary French climber Gaston Rébuffat wrote of his time there: 'On this sinister, murderous face, the rusty piton and rotten ropes dating from the early attempts, the stone wall which surrounded us as we ate, and which sheltered Sedlmayer and Mehringer before they died, all combined to remind us that the moment you cease climbing toward the summit, success and safety itself are compromised.'

That day, our third on the Eiger, began badly for my mental state because, expecting to continue heading in an upwards direction, we actually had to move diagonally downwards across an extremely steep slope, the Third Ice-Field, to the base of a crucial feature known as the Ramp. This 700-foot-high, left-slanting gash, overhung by walls of limestone, contained many nasty surprises.

I had read much about the Ramp, which some Eiger pundits describe as the most technically difficult section on the wall, with little to hold on to with either hand or foot. Twice over the next few hours, inching up the central chimney of the Ramp, I came within an ace of falling, but on each occasion, my axes caught hold on some tiny unseen nub and halted my downward rush. There were icy chimneys, awkward rock slabs, tricky and frightening overhangs and side-pulls, hand-palming off sloping holds, and the occasional hand-jamb. Near the upper reaches of the great gully there were two or three stretches of rock that nearly defeated my every attempt. Looking down at any point during the

Ramp climb would have been a big mistake, as the airy ice-fields immediately below had a hypnotic effect. Looking up was not to be recommended either, in the Ramp's narrower reaches, for then my rucksack lid's contents would jab the back of my neck.

Somewhere on the Ramp in 1961, an Austrian climber with a brilliant repertoire of ultra-severe Alpine ascents, the twenty-two-year-old Adolf Mayr, came to grief attempting the first ever solo attempt of the face. Down in Grindelwald, queues of tourists waited their turn to gawp at 'Adi' through the hotel telescopes. Somewhere in the mid-section, at a spot named the Waterfall Chimney, he needed to traverse across wet rock. Watchers below saw him hack at a foothold with his axe. Then he stepped sideways, missed his footing and fell 4,000 feet to his death.

Above the Ramp there were sections of slippery ice and treacherous patches of soft snow into which neither my axes nor my crampons could be trusted to hold firm. By always checking that I had three reasonable holds before advancing a leg or arm to a fourth higher hold, none of the many slips that I made proved disastrous, merely heart-stopping at the time.

Unbeknown to me, both my companions had been concerned that the Ramp might prove too technically difficult for my meagre rock-ability and that the expedition would end there. Ian recorded on his camera tape that evening: 'The Ramp is about three pitches high, or three rope-lengths high, and the most difficult bit is the final rope-length. There is no ice which would give good purchase for the axes, it's only rock. It is very steep in places and it's also overhanging. That pushes you out and, with the rucksack, all the weight is on your arms. You are looking for features either side on the wall, and they are pretty smooth in places, so you are scratching on tiny holds to get up. Ran is doing excellently;

today was probably the point at which he could have failed. He managed to do it very well, so we were very pleased.'

At one belay I met up with Ian just below a single boulder the size of half a standard UK red postbox. As we conversed, a rock struck the boulder and shattered into shards, one of which struck me hard on the helmet. The rest passed harmlessly over our heads. Here we ran out of ice at a place of much loose slate aptly named the Brittle Ledges.

For a while I could find no way up one layer of slate, for every rock I tried to use for a hold simply broke off. My axes were no help. Eventually I had to remove my mitts and bury my bad hand deep into a vertical cleft to achieve the needed purchase. This move coincided with the failure of my last available hand-warmer pouch. Resupplies, deep in my rucksack, were unobtainable and my hand soon grew numb with cold. This was bad timing because, above the Brittle Ledges, Ian led up a vertical wall of slate about ninety feet high. Maybe I was too tired to think clearly, or perhaps my cold, numb left hand, incapable of gripping anything but my ice-axe (and that thanks only to the crutch of its wrist loop), left me pretty much one-armed at the time.

Whatever the reason, I worked harder and with greater desperation on that single ninety-foot wall than on any previous part of the North Face. Despite the brittle nature of the rock, the first few yards up from a little snow-covered ledge on to the Brittle Crack were overhanging. The upper twelve feet involved an appallingly exposed traverse around a corner with space shouting at you from every direction. The tiny cracks and sparse piton placements available for my axes disappeared as I neared the top. All apparent handhold bulges were smooth and sloped downwards, and my bare fingers simply slid off them. My arms and my legs began to shake, my biceps to burn. Pure luck got me to the ice-patch that capped the wall, into which I sank an axe with great relief and hauled myself up, a wreck, to the tiny snow ledge where a grinning Ian was belayed.

'This is it,' he said. 'We spend the night here. Lovely view.'

A bit of axe-burrowing formed a fairly comfortable ledge for the three of us, and again the mental stress and physical toil of the day overcame my worries about that drop a few inches away from my sleeping position. I lost a mitt off the ledge during the night, but I had a spare immediately available.

Again the mental stress and physical toil of the day overcame my worries about that drop a few inches away from my sleeping position.

I had just spent three days ascending by far the most difficult climb of my admittedly short climbing life, and yet, by repute, the worst lay ahead.

On the morning of our fourth day on the face, I woke with a dry mouth and butterflies fluttering about in my stomach. Joe Simpson's professional description of the Traverse of the Gods was clear in my mind, '5,000 feet of clean air' whistling beneath and very poor opportunities for strong piton holds, all compounded by a very tough bit of climbing at the end of the traverse, close to the legendary Spider.

In the valley below, veteran climber Stephen Venables, who had climbed the North Face over twenty years before, watched our every move through binoculars. He wrote: 'Taking crampons repeatedly on and off is not an option, so Ran had to tread with steel points on snow, ice and bare rock.

Above the Spider.

Terrified of damaging the shortened fingers of his left hand, he kept his mitts on, gripping as best he could. He knew that if he fell, he would go for a huge swing over the void before the rope held him.'

Ian was behind me as I stepped out along this hellish cliffside, and he described his thoughts thus: 'It's dramatic, nervy climbing for experienced climbers, but for someone like Ran who suffers from vertigo, it can easily become a complete nightmare. The rock here is loose, covered in verglas in winter and frighteningly exposed. In fact, at one point your heels overhang the whole drop of the wall to the snows of Kleine Scheidegg below.'

Suddenly, well ahead of me, and appearing to be glued to the sheer wall merely by his fingertips and booted toes, Kenton disappeared around an abrupt corner. For no good reason this unsettled me badly. Behind me, Ian observed my reactions: 'He is no drama queen, so I didn't expect him to break down sobbing, but by the methodical and calm way he worked across the first half of the traverse, he looked to be in complete control. Once Ran had disappeared out of sight, I packed up my cameras and began climbing. It soon became evident that all was not as well as it seemed on the surface. I can't repeat Kenton's comments here, but it was a classic example of what is known in British Alpine circles as a "Kentrum" – the toys were well outside the pram. The issue seemed to be that, caught out of rope, Kenton had been forced to take a belay on two pathetic rotting bits of tat. Ran, swinging round to the second half of the traverse, felt the full impact of the sickening exposure and suffered an attack of the vertigo he had so far successfully kept at bay. Reeling in their own worlds, a frank exchange of views followed.'

Ian's interpretation of events was close to the mark. Something snapped as soon as I rounded the sharp bend in the wall. I may have inadvertently allowed myself a glimpse downwards beyond my normally carefully regimented focus point – my crampon points and not an inch beyond them. The onrush of sheer terror that this error sparked coincided with a tightening of the rope between me and the still invisible Kenton. 'Give me slack,' I shouted. I had the rope back to Ian jammed behind me round an ice-nub. I had to retreat a yard to loosen it. I was teetering on my front points on a mere rock scratch. I was terrified. My voice rose to a bellow.

'GIVE ME SLACK!'

This brought a furious response from my unseen leader. Furious, but to me unintelligible, so I had no idea what his problem was, no idea that his position was precarious. He knew that, if I fell at that moment, he was unlikely to be able to maintain a hold on the mountain. He was desperately doing his best to drive ice-screws in to improve his belay point. The last thing he wanted to do was to give me slack.

After an age, or so it seemed, I felt slack rope from Kenton, reached back to flick Ian's rope free, and crept onwards above that sickening drop until I could see the still muttering Kenton perched on a patch of naked ice. There was nobody, not even Ian, who I trusted so completely in what, to me, was the most frightening environment on Earth. Without Kenton, I could never have even contemplated setting foot on the Eiger's North Face. And here, of course, is another key lesson about fear. Facing it alone is one thing. The key is to have the courage to share your fears with somone you trust, to ask for help and accept it.

We moved fairly quickly up the steep hard ice of the White Spider, so called due to its shape – a blob of white ice with white gullies stretching up and down from its centre for hundreds of feet. In bad weather, detritus from above can turn the Spider into a death zone for any climber caught on its face.

At a belay, Kenton helped me take off my windproof jacket, but I fumbled and lost my grip on it. A breeze grabbed it and, in an instant, it slid away down the slope, gathering speed. A bad item to lose at that height on the Eiger. We still had 1,000 feet to go, straight up a maze of intricate gullies, the notorious Exit Cracks, the final chimney of which included two rope-lengths up a near-vertical ice staircase with the treads all sloping the wrong way.

From the White Spider on, there were many obstacles that would, back in the Avon Gorge or on the Welsh sea-cliffs, have been too much for my inadequate technical skills and lack of upper body strength. But this was the last rock problem I would face. The summit was tantalisingly close, so I attacked each new problem as though my life depended upon it. Perhaps it did. The walls on both sides of various grooves and chimneys were smooth, featureless and often at eighty degrees.

The nightmare of the Exit Cracks ended with a great pendulum traverse, way to the left of our previous axis of ascent, a long icy chute, and a treacherous bulge of mixed shale and snow, both ingredients being unpleasantly loose underfoot. The evening sun was welcoming as we emerged from the last of the gullies. I craned my neck, arching my back, and saw a wonderful swathe of open sky where for four long days I had seen only the ever-rising, dark wall of the Eiger. Above us now was only a steep wall of snow and ice leading up to the knife-edge cornice of the summit ridge, and by dusk we had reached it, but were still some thirty minutes and 300 yards below the actual summit further along the Mittellegi Ridge where Kenton selected a nook on the far, southern side of the cornice, and where we spent an hour digging out a platform for the sleeping bags. Ian's notes recorded: 'We had an awful night. There was no reception on the mobile so we couldn't communicate with anyone or do the live broadcast. Then I dropped the ITV camera over the edge – but we were so knackered and it was so cold. It was a spectacular ridge to the summit, so it was a really nice finish. I'm pretty proud of what we have done. Particularly for Ran.'

We left the bivouac at 9.30 a.m. and threaded our way towards the summit along a classic knife-edge ridge. Ian wrote: 'Kenton led us with Ran in the middle and myself last in our little line. I was acutely aware that if Ran began sliding down one side of the ridge, it was my job to throw myself off the opposite side of the mountain, arresting our fall in a see-saw effect.'

At 10 a.m. on the fifth day of our climb we reached the summit – thanks entirely to the brilliance and the patience (usually!) of Kenton and Ian. Within half an hour of our arrival there, an evil-looking cloud bank raced over the mountain ranges to the south, soon to envelop the Eiger. Our weather forecasters had got it dead right. As we descended down the easy side of the ridge I felt deliriously happy to be back on comparative terra firma and I made up my mind to steer clear of all mountains in the future . . . probably. It was great to learn that within a week of our return, our friends at Marie Curie had already raised £1.4 million towards our £1.5-million target, with hopes that our Marie Curie Eiger Challenge Appeal would top out at well over £3 million before it closed down.

▲

So what did my ascent of the fearsome Eiger teach me? Perhaps only that I would never truly beat my vertigo, just manage it when forced to. My training for the Eiger with Kenton was gradual in the extreme, and I somehow got through the whole experience – but thinking back on the

Ian Parnell, edging to the summit.

feat later, it was clear to me that I only really lost my fear of heights when I had those two guys with me. Even as I reached the top of the North Face, I knew that I would never do it again.

Two years later, on the farm on Exmoor with my wife Louise, I remember seeing how the trees had dropped leaves in the guttering that autumn. Clearly something must be done to clear them out. So naturally I turned to Louise and said, 'Well, I'll hold the ladder and you go up . . .'

CHAPTER EIGHT

▲

MORTALITY

You don't need to visit the polar regions to risk
sudden death. You may well be run over
outside Tesco tomorrow.

Ginny Fiennes

Life has to go on.

Early in 2003 I knew that I needed a complete break and change of activity, so, out of the blue, I phoned Mike Stroud and suggested that we get involved in another expedition. He was, however, too busy in Southampton to spare the three months an average expedition would take. His counter-suggestion was that we run seven marathons, one on each of the world's seven continents, over seven consecutive days. This was an idea originally proposed by Mary Gadams, his American teammate on a previous Eco-Challenge race, but she had not managed to get the enterprise off the ground. The idea appealed to me enormously and Mike and I set about getting the sponsorship and logistics in place while training seriously for the running. We would need to start in Antarctica and it would be good to aim to finish by joining an official marathon run in somewhere like New York. It was only a case of connecting it all up.

The day after I finished the final corrections to the text of my biography of Captain Scott, I was due to give a talk to a convention in Dunblane, so I told Ginny that I would see her the following morning and I drove to Bristol Airport, arriving at the departure desk in good time. I boarded the aircraft and settled down to read a magazine. I can remember nothing that happened from that moment for the next three days and nights.

Apparently not more than a few minutes before take-off I collapsed noiselessly and was dragged into the aisle, where a passenger with medical training gave me instant mouth-to-mouth resuscitation. The pilot called the fire service, and the fire engine accelerated across the tarmac to drop off two firemen recently trained in the use of the mobile defibrillator which they carried on board. They applied a powerful 200-joule DC electric shock, which passed right across my chest to depolarise every cell in my heart. This caused my natural pacemaker to recover and my heart was once more a regularly beating pump. Deeply unconscious, I was then rushed to a waiting ambulance. Twice more on the journey to Bristol's Royal Infirmary and three more times in the Accident and Emergency unit I lapsed back into fibrillation. The stabilising drugs I was given proved ineffective but the doctors managed in due course to stabilise my condition. Fearful, however, that I would have further attacks, they sent me to surgery. Within just two hours of my initial collapse, I was on cardiac bypass with a machine artificially pumping and refrigerating my blood.

A consultant cardiologist, Dr Tim Cripps, commented to me much later that out of the hundred thousand people a year in the UK who have a cardiac arrest, the first and only warning they get is the attack itself and only very few are lucky enough to be near a defibrillator and someone who knows how to use it. After treating me to some examples of others who had not been so lucky, he went on, 'When you arrived in our ICU you were measured at three points on the Glasgow Coma Scale. The lowest the scale goes is Level Three, which Richard Hammond of *Top Gear* achieved after his car crash at 260 mph.'

Dr Cripps called the senior Bristol cardiac surgeon, Gianni Angelini, who subsequently wrote: 'On arrival RF had a coronary angiography which showed the presence of a large thrombus (blood clot) blocking the left anterior descending and the intermediary arteries, two of the most important arteries of the heart. He was fully anaesthetised, artificially ventilated and taken at once to the operating theatre. I was informed at my home and when I arrived was told it was quite bad . . . The situation was so urgent that we decided to go ahead and open his chest even prior to the arrival of the perfusion team . . . Two bypass grafts were performed, one using an artery called the internal mammary artery, which is behind the breastbone, the other a long segment of vein from the leg. There was serious concern about his neurological state since we didn't know the extent and duration of his cardiac arrest at the airport and thereafter. He was kept sedated for twenty-four hours . . . Then woken up . . . From then on it became rather difficult to manage him, since he virtually refused any analgesia, saying that he did not have a great deal of pain. And that he wanted the tubes and lines removed as soon as possible because he had to walk up and down the corridor. He was discharged five days after surgery.'

My chest had been opened up from top to bottom and later sewn up with silver wire.

Ginny had sat by my bedside day and night and watched my tube-fed, artificially ticking body, blood-smeared in places, lying in front of her for more than three days. Every now and again a nurse would enter and thump my knee or foot for a reaction. None came. This could not have been a good time for Ginny. When I eventually came to, we kissed as best we could and she told me that I had had a heart attack. It took a while to work out what she was saying and where I was. My chest had been opened up from top to bottom and later sewn up with silver wire, the knots of which I can still feel jutting proud just beneath my skin.

Leaning on Ginny's shoulder, once the pipes and tubes had all been removed from various places, I managed to walk a few paces, though I felt extremely sore. Ginny drove me home with strict instructions not to let me move.

Why, we both wondered, had I had this attack at all? Ultimately, as Mike Stroud has since written, my cumulative risk factors simply overcame the protection of what was, for my age, a very high level of physical fitness. It was probably always going to happen, though having been in intensive care, any idea of joining Mike on his marathon challenge was surely out of the question.

▲

Death has always been a possibility in my chosen career, but I do not dwell on it when I am on expeditions, any more than I dwell on it in my day-to-day life. Much as with fear in general, I prefer to stuff all thoughts of danger to the back of my mind rather than lying awake at night thinking about the end. I think of my next handhold on a climb rather than the drop. I think of placing my next step firmly, rather than the crevasse that may lie beneath it.

I think of placing my next step firmly, rather than the crevasse that may lie beneath it.

In short, I switch from the general to the specific. It's not 'I might die doing this', it's 'Am I taking my pills correctly, and should I see another doctor?' These days I have to have my ears cleaned out, which I do every three months to avoid my wife Louise saying, 'Stop saying WHAT!' It's a task I have to do, no more, no less. I don't fixate on it as a sign that I am ageing.

The heart attack in 2003 did clarify one thing for me, however. Throughout my career I have often been asked, especially since my daughter Elizabeth was born, if I felt guilty risking my life on my expeditions. Having survived the heart attack – and being aware it could happen again at any moment, while making a cup of tea just as much as being halfway up a mountain – militates against any feelings of guilt.

Additionally, I know that my wife Louise is a truly wonderful mother, as mine was, and I grew up without a father. To this day, although I hugely respect his memory, I have never emotionally missed him, for I never knew him, and Elizabeth, who was not yet one year old at the time of my attempt on the Eiger, would certainly not remember me. Both Ginny and Louise married me in the full knowledge that I make a living through expeditions and intend to do so as long as I can. So I could feel no more guilt than would, say, a miner or truck driver, both professions with far higher death rates than mine.

▲

The day we returned to England after our attempt to run seven marathons, on seven continents, in seven days (see Chapter 9), a press conference was held by the British Heart Foundation. I said goodbye to Mike Stroud and his family and was given a lift back to Exmoor by a friend. On reaching Exford village, just over a mile from home, I saw a big banner flying high over the road by the village green, and, below it, a crowd of people. We stopped as local folk, many of whom I knew well, surrounded the car and cheered and clapped. The banner was a *Welcome Home, Ran* sign. I looked around for Ginny and spotted her with our two dogs. She wore her lovely warm smile of welcome, but looked both tired and thin. Later that evening, sitting by the log fire at Greenlands as we had

Ginny in her prime, manning the radio in Camp Alert, 1982.

so often done over the past twenty years, she told me her news and my stomach churned with dread. She might have cancer.

Ginny had, over many years, had sudden stomach pains at no particular time and for no known or obvious reason. We had both put this down to twisted Fallopian tubes, or some other birth-connected condition. We had seen our doctor and specialists about the pain intermittently after especially bad attacks, but these were thankfully rare, to the point that sometimes a year would pass without one. Or so I assumed. Maybe Ginny did not always tell me when it happened. The doctors never found anything specifically wrong with her. Ginny had suffered two especially bad pains in the lower stomach area whilst I was away on the seven marathons and she had been driven to Taunton hospital, an hour from home, for a check-up and painkillers.

The specialists confirmed that she had a virulent form of stomach cancer which was spreading fast. She must have chemotherapy sessions every week for at least three months and starting at once. In between them we could live at home.

We spent Christmas on Exmoor with Ginny's family and with many of our best friends visiting from time to time.

I could not remember any time in my adult life when she was not the reason for the glow in my heart when we were together, and the longed-for safe haven during my wanderings without her. I was desperate not to lose her and thankful for any tiny spark of hope that our doctor might murmur.

By the second month, January 2004, Ginny was seldom able to leave the house, other than by ambulance for treatment. We were assigned a doctor in Exeter Hospital who specialised in cancer treatment. But the various chemotherapy treatments did not work and the disease spread. Later that month Ginny moved into an NHS cancer ward shared with some seven other ladies. She made friends quickly with many of them and with many of the nurses. I spent every day at her bedside or wheeling her about in a chair. At night I slept in a spare upstairs room in the hospital. Ginny's sister, Abby, would drive down from Liverpool as often as she could and many friends were frequent visitors, but Ginny's health diminished inexorably as the disease spread into her key organs. She had emergency operations and I sat outside the theatres startled by every unusual noise from within.

Three months after her diagnosis, Ginny was moved to the hospice close to the hospital. I was allowed to sleep in a spare room in the hospice.

Many friends and Ginny's family came on her last day alive to show their love for her. But her pain became ever worse, and towards evening the nurses had to increase her morphine drip above the previous levels. Abby and my niece, Beelie, were with me as Ginny faded slowly. I could not control my misery. She died and escaped further pain.

Over the previous week we had sometimes prayed together with the friendly and sincere hospice chaplain. Once Ginny held me tightly and thanked me for our life together, using wonderful words that I will never forget.

Abby and my great friend Anton came back to Greenlands and stayed with me. Together we planned Ginny's funeral and memorial service and, months later, we held a gathering of her friends, over 700 people, at the celebration of her life at the Royal Geographical Society, the place where she had spent many long hours in the dusty archives with maps and books researching for our expeditions.

Three months after Ginny died I could bear things no more. I was becoming morose, inactive and full of self-pity.

I tried to lift my head above the deep ache of Ginny's death and tell myself that she would be wanting me to attack

▲

Each of us, in our brief lifespan,
has the chance to spend our time
in sadness or in joy.

_____

life again, to 'get on with it', to 'be dangerous': all her little catch phrases. I found boxes of all the notes and letters she had sent me down the years since long before we married. I read them all again when alone in our bedroom. Then I filed them in boxes and sent them to Abby for safe-keeping because, at the time, I felt and wished that I would die.

Sometimes I would say to myself that everybody will sooner or later lose or be lost by their loved ones, but life has to go on. I would argue to myself that every one of the billions of people who have ever lived have been sad to some degree at some time. I remembered walking with Ginny, Anton and his wife Jill down the 1.5-kilometre-long death tunnels of the Paris catacombs. We passed by six million neatly stacked skulls. Each and every one had had, during their brief lifespan, the chance to spend time in sadness or in joy. I thought, too, of how lucky I was to have known such love and to have been with Ginny during the last months when she needed me. Now, with Ginny gone, as well as my mother and two of my sisters, I was still alive, if only just, cardiac-wise, so I had to get on with life. Not vegetate for even a moment.

I knew I must break out of my own cage of misery and I remembered an Everest climb invitation I had received a year before from Sibusiso Vilane in Swaziland, the first Black person ever to summit Everest. I needed a sharp jolt and what could provide one better than one of life's ultimate challenges. The highest mountain on Earth would surely drag me out of the dark void of my current existence.

I wrote to Sibu. He was delighted, and accepted the fact that I would first have to learn how to climb (this was before my torturous attempt on the Eiger). He suggested doing so through a UK mountain tours company called Jagged Globe. I called them at once, but their boss explained that they could not take anybody and everybody up Everest and, with due respect, I was 'sixty, cardiac-challenged and missing some digits'. He suggested that I join two of Jagged Globe's mountaineering courses. First there was a ten-day Alpine peaks instructional tour to see if I could cope with the basics of snow and ice-climbing. Then, if I received a reasonable report from the Alps guide, I should progress to their Ecuador Volcanoes tour, involving climbs up to 20,000 feet, which would introduce me to the effects of high altitude on my system. This was especially important because of my cardiac history.

▲

With Everest to aim for and provide me with a purpose, I took on as much work as I could and averaged four conference lectures a week. I loved Greenlands, but the sadness and loneliness returned each time I went back. Ginny had told me many times over the years that, should she die before me, I was to remarry as soon as possible. I had said the same to her.

At a lecture I had given to the Chester branch of the Royal Geographical Society the previous summer, I had met one of their members, Louise Millington, and had since taken her out when she was not busy with the horse transporting company she had built up based in her Cheshire home. She was thirty-six years old, full of life, mercurial, and she jolted me out of my miserable state. We agreed to marry in March 2005 and honeymoon at the Everest Base Camp in Tibet.

Abby, Ginny's closest relative, said to the press: 'Ran has been a much-loved member of our family for nearly fifty years and always will be. He and Ginny had an exceptionally happy marriage and were in love with each other for all their adult lives. Ran was devastated by Ginny's illness and death and he has had a desperately long, lonely year without her. To see him happy again with Louise is wonderful. He still grieves

Above: With Louise at ALERT (the African Lion Ecological and Research Trust).

Left: Footsore at Base Camp.

for Ginny and nothing will change or diminish his feelings for my sister. But Ginny wouldn't want Ran to be sad or lonely She urged him to marry again and everyone in the family is one hundred per cent supportive of his decision We all wish Ran and Louise every happiness.'

During the last month before going to Everest, I discovered that I could not properly hold a standard ice-axe in my frost-damaged left hand. So we went to DMM, a climbing gear factory in Wales, where they sponsored me with a special axe with a thin shaft as well as a steel hook for, hopefully, gripping those tiny holds that my half-fingers could not manage.

The seventh of March was my sixty-first birthday. Five days later Louise and I were married, and a fortnight after that we left Heathrow bound for Kathmandu in Nepal. At the airport a reporter from The Times interviewed Louise and asked her all the usual questions. She admitted that she was worried about the altitude and the strain on my heart.

We spent two weeks in the Everest Base Camp at 5,200 metres (17,060 feet), sometimes trudging a few miles upwards on the Everest trail or back downhill to the Rongbuk Monastery. Acclimatisation was the main aim of our existence. Louise suffered severe headaches, but stayed with me for a fortnight before returning to England just before our Chief Guide decided that we were ready to try our first trek up to the Advance Base Camp. Our gear was taken by sixty-five yaks with drivers who whistled and yelled at their animals when the trail was especially narrow or slippery.

I knew that all 2005 summit bids had to be completed by the first week of June because that was the annual date for the arrival of the monsoon winds which would make Everest lethal to climbers. I still had about fifty days in which to reach the top and thereby, I hoped, enable the British Heart Foundation to raise our £2-million target. I also had a personal pet hope. For twenty-three years I had competed with Norwegians for polar firsts. Now I had a chance of going for another. Only a handful of individuals had managed to cross both Antarctica and the Arctic Ocean. Børge Ousland was one of them, and he had tried to add Everest to his trophy list. Sibu had been with him when he had decided to turn round not far short of the summit. So I hoped that my heart and my lungs would behave themselves for the next fifty days. Weather permitting, I might then raise my £2 million *and* beat the Norwegians. Wishful thinking, I realised, but there was no harm in hoping.

For years I had competed with Norwegians for polar firsts. Now I had a chance of going for another.

I slept well that night at the first interim camp at 5,500 metres (18,045 feet) en route to Advance Base, and next morning our group moved on up the glacial valley, an ascent of 950 metres with sharkfin pinnacles of ice towering above each side of the trail, known as the Magic Highway. We crossed or skirted lakes of frozen meltwater, great glaciers curved down from high valleys to join ours, but all, we knew, were shrinking, the main glacier by over a hundred vertical feet in the past ten years alone. I kept up with the others without trouble, and after five hours came to the tents of the second interim camp at 6,088 metres (approximately 20,000 feet).

I slotted my sleeping bag, boots and rucksack between the two other Brits, Ian and Jens – by chance, not chauvinistic intention – and welcomed a cup of tea proffered by Ian.

We were all dog-tired and most of us had headaches since, despite our cautious acclimatisation to date, we were for the first time living and working well above 17,000 feet where the human body starts to deteriorate, indeed to rot. It literally consumes itself for energy. Sleeping becomes a problem, muscle wasting and weight loss take place, and this process of deterioration continues more quickly, the higher the altitude. Scientific advice by 2005 strongly recommended that nobody should stay at that height for more than an absolute maximum of ten days and that, at or above 26,000 feet, the so-called Death Zone, acclimatisation is not possible.

We camped at 6,460 metres (21,200 feet), higher than I had ever been. So far, I thanked God for small mercies, I appeared to have escaped retinal damage, severe headaches, heart pains, cerebral and pulmonary oedema, tensions with my fellow climbers, and even the hacking Khumbu cough that racked many climbers even down at Base Camp. Periodic breathing, or Cheyne-Stokes syndrome, would only affect me if I slept or dozed without oxygen, so my summit chances were still intact.

The Times journalist who had been sent out to cover the entire climb, wrote cynical articles, humorous in a caustic sort of way, that covered most aspects of life at the camps . . .

There are normal people on Everest, but the proportion of glory-hunters is abnormally high when compared with that at sea level. As a BBC compère might say: if you liked 'Fame Academy', then you'll LOVE 'Advance Base Camp'. They're all here, the star-struck and the fame-chasers, with their promotional stickers and funny logo'ed hats, their business cards and Americanised pidgin English, and for a journalist there is just nowhere to hide from these people – all want front-page coverage,

preferably in *The Times*. So far I have met the sirdar who is to guide Tom Cruise up the mountain next year, the prospective first Punjabi woman and the first Bhutanese man to climb Everest. There is the bloke from Australia whose aim is to be the first one-armed Australian on the summit, and another man who claims that he will be the first asthmatic to have reached the top.

Why do these trophy-hunters annoy me so much? And doesn't Ranulph Fiennes fall into the same category? In answer to question two: absolutely not. Fiennes is one of the most self-effacing, focused people here and is climbing Everest only to raise £2 million for charity: he talks about almost nothing else.

My Sherpa, Boca Lama, and I tried to get ready for our night in this so-called Death Camp, unpacking our rucksacks and checking our oxygen systems without upsetting each other's space, all in a tiny two-man tent pitched on rocks and ice. Any item that escaped through the entry door was liable to slide, then fall for many thousands of feet to the snow terraces and glaciers below. Various dead bodies had been found in the tents here, including an Indian climber the previous week.

Sibu nearly died that day after reaching the summit when his oxygen ran out, although we did not know this until the following morning when one of our Sherpas found him slouched beside the trail. Various stories of recent happenings reached us on the walkie-talkie system or through other climbers. A few days earlier, when a Slovenian died on the summit ridge, a solo climber from Bhutan, close by him, ran out of oxygen and began to hallucinate due to hypoxia. He wandered by one of the old corpses near to the fixed rope, probably the one with green boots that most climbers remember, and thought he saw the corpse pointing at an object nearby. This turned out to be a half-snow-buried orange oxygen cylinder. The Bhutani, to his joy, found that there was still oxygen in it, clipped it to his system and survived to tell his tale to everyone in Advance Base.

From the Death Camp, the final climb ascends and traverses a steep stretch of striated limestone, known as the Yellow Band, mostly by way of a part-snow-filled gully where many old ropes can cause confusion, especially since this section must be done at night. However, the great motivating thought is that from the tents to the summit ridge is a mere 300 metres in height.

So why on earth do people choose to risk their lives on Everest year after year? I can only speak for myself. First, to raise money for charity; and second, with both Poles conquered, the mighty peak of the Himalayas remains as the greatest conquest available to the explorer.

I struggled into my boots, pack and oxygen system, said goodbye to Ian and the other three, and, with Boca Lama a few yards behind, grinning as usual, began the fairly steep climb up the fixed ropes with new batteries in my head torch. In seven or eight hours, on a fixed rope the whole way, I hoped to be on the summit of Everest. We moved off into the night, pitch black beyond the cone of our torch lights. There were slippery rocks, snow patches and a bewildering choice of upward-leading ropes, some frayed almost through, others brand new. In the torch light it paid to take time. I found myself panting far more than on the previous climb, despite taking it slowly, perhaps because of the gradient. I felt cold despite the exertion, and I felt dizzy, too. Something was wrong but nothing I could identify, so I kept going in a stop-start way, gasping for breath every few metres. Then, some forty minutes after setting out, my world caved in.

Somebody, it seemed, had clamped powerful arms around my chest and was squeezing the life out of me. And the surgical wire that held my ribs together felt as though it was tearing through my chest. My thoughts were simple: I am having another heart attack. I will be dead in minutes. No defibrillator on hand this time. Then I remembered that Louise had pestered me to carry special pills – Glycerine Tri-Nitrate (GTN). You put one under your tongue, where it fizzes and causes your system to dilate in all the right places. I tore at my jacket pocket and, removing my mitts, crammed at least six tablets under my tongue before swallowing.

I clung to the rope, hanging out over the great drop and waiting to die. My one glimpse of Boca Lama, who said nothing, was of his usual big grin as my torch lit up his features. Five minutes later I was still alive. The tablets, I knew, could, if you were lucky, stave off a heart attack and give you time to get to a cardiac unit. They are *not* a means of avoiding an attack in order to allow you to continue climbing. This might not be my own end, but it *was* definitely the signal to descend to lower altitudes at once.

Some twenty minutes later we were back down in the Death Camp. There was no tent to enter as our group were in the act of booting and kitting up, using all available tent space. So I waited outside with Boca Lama until Ian and the others had disappeared up into the night.

'I must go down quickly,' I told Boca Lama. He shook his head and the grin disappeared. It would, he explained, be too dangerous to descend until we could 'see our feet'. This meant dawn in five hours' time. I knew my best hope of survival, as had been the case on Kilimanjaro, was to lose height rapidly. The tightness had gone from my chest, but the sharp discomfort around the stitch-wires was still there. I contemplated going on down without Boca Lama, but decided against it. Going up an icy, slippery, steep slope in the darkness is a lot safer than descending one. Statistically, the vast majority of accidents happen on the descent. The concentration of going up seems to disappear to be replaced by a weary nonchalance. Nothing matters apart from a longing for warmth and comfort. Lost in these thoughts you become careless. The focus gone and the mind weary, it is all too easy to lose your footing or clip carelessly into a rope. Three thousand metres of void awaited directly below our tent.

Nine-times Everest climber Ed Viesturs has two favourite sayings: 'Just because you love the mountains doesn't mean the mountains love you'; and 'Getting to the top is optional. Getting down is mandatory.'

Dawn came eventually and we descended without a break to the North Col, where we rested for two hours. My Everest was over. If I had feared a scathing reaction from our *Times* correspondent, I was pleasantly surprised: 'Aborting his climb will be seen by the mountain community as a wise and courageous decision. Duncan Chessell, who has led thirty-five Himalayan expeditions, said, 'For a sixty-year-old man to make it even this far is extraordinary. You would expect only fifty per cent of climbers to reach anywhere near this high, especially during this season.'

I congratulated my fellow Jagged Globe climbers, especially Sibu, and within a day I was back down in Base Camp. Forty-eight hours after that I was checked out in Harley Street for new cardiac damage. None was evident, so it is likely that, on Everest and previously on Kilimanjaro, I had mere angina warnings. What would have happened if I had not heeded them or had not had the GTN tablets, it is impossible to know. I learned later that on the other side of the mountain a Scottish climber, forty-year-old Robert Milne, died of a heart attack on the same night and at the same height as I had my attack. I assume that he had no GTN pills with him.

The tangible declared aim of my Everest attempt, all costs of which were sponsored by the generosity of Paul Sykes, had been to raise £2 million for an MRI Scanner Unit and Catheter Laboratory in the Great Ormond Street Hospital for Children in London. The British Heart Foundation eventually raised the £2 million through the Ran Fiennes Healthy Hearts Appeal, despite my failure on the mountain, and I cut the ribbon to officially open the gleaming new clinic. Its purpose is purely for heart research, and it will enable BHF medical professionals to explore the heart disease that affects children, helping them to develop new interventional techniques with the aim of saving young lives.

Since our 'honeymoon' at the Everest Base Camp had been a non-event, Louise and I took up the kind offer of John Costello, who had checked out my lungs prior to Everest, to stay for a week in his family villa in southern Spain. A couple of months later Louise told me that she was pregnant and, on Easter Day 2006, our daughter Elizabeth gave her first yell. A month later I was sixty-two years old and changed my first nappy.

CHAPTER NINE

▲

PERSEVERANCE

Just. Keep. Going.

Ranulph Fiennes

▲

What else is life, if not the

ability to overcome?

———

As with so many things in life, the ability to *just keep going* is of paramount importance. My own physical challenges have always been chosen by me and entered into willingly. The same cannot be said, in ordinary life, of the loss of a loved one, the failing of one's health or the loss of freedom felt by so many when the Pandemic hit in March 2020. But what else is life, if not the ability to overcome; the will to continue to push past the barriers in our path and to reach the goals we set ourselves? I feel that as keenly now, in my seventy-eighth year, planning to zigzag around the country on my next lecture tour, as I did leaning into the straps of my sledge with Mike Stroud thirty years ago in our attempt to complete the first ever crossing of Antarctica on foot and without outside support.

▲

Charlie Burton had summoned me to the Royal Geographical Society to study a proposal he and Oliver Shepard had put together for such an expedition. I pointed out the indisputable evidence that neither man, nor machine, nor pack animal (huskies included) could carry sufficient food and fuel to cross Antarctica from coast to coast.

'No machine devised by man –' I poked Charlie in the stomach by way of emphasis – 'is fuel-efficient enough to make such a distance without resupply. The Americans and Soviets have both tried and failed. And since neither machines nor dog-teams can make it, humans man-hauling sledges are out of the question. It is quite clear that Scott's greatest error was in trying to man-haul.'

'Balls,' Charlie pointed out helpfully. 'Scott was absolutely right in reckoning manpower to be the most efficient method. Our journey will prove it.'

The two of them showed me their plan and I was forced to concede that it seemed to make sense. And as Ollie added, 'If *we* don't do the journey, somebody else will.'

He knew my Achilles heel.

I researched previous attempts at unsupported manhaul journeys in Antarctica. An Anglo-Canadian group led by Briton Roger Mear had just managed, in seventy-five days, to make it as far as the Pole, but they were then airlifted out. Their attempt was the most successful journey to date, but Charlie's proposal involved twice the distance.

While involved in the Ubar search, I had made a few tentative moves to set up the Antarctica crossing attempt. Prince Charles had agreed to be its patron and suggested that we use it to raise funds for multiple sclerosis. Back in 1990, at his behest, we had raised £2,300,000 and had helped to set up Europe's first MS research centre in Cambridge. A further major success would bolster the centre's achievements.

Our preparations progressed slowly until, in May 1991, one of Ollie's 'KGB informants in Norway' warned us that Erling Kagge, our most active polar rival at the time, was announcing to the Scandinavian media his intention to cross the Antarctic continent in 1992.

I knew Kagge was an exceptionally strong cross-country skier, and speed with endurance were the keys to success in Antarctica. Neither Ollie nor Charlie, though 100 per cent dependable, were keen on pushing themselves to the limits. I decided to confront this issue at once and, explaining my Kagge worries, I suggested we ask the highly competitive Mike Stroud to join our team.

Not long afterwards Ollie called to say that he and Charlie had both decided to change their roles. 'We would want to enjoy the crossing,' he explained. 'Once you get competitive any signs of enjoyment are tantamount to mutiny.' So, they took on the role of the organisers, and Mike agreed to join the field team on the condition that he would conduct an extensive scientific research programme throughout the journey.

Whatever business you are in, it is bad practice to allow your chief rival to have a clear run at a main prize without even mounting a challenge.

The challenge that faced us involved very exact timing because the Antarctic travel season does not last long. The mathematics were very simple. We must each tow a start-out load of almost 500 pounds, at least sixteen miles a day for 108 days. Since this was a performance well in excess of any man-hauling achievement in history, Mike agreed that there was every likelihood that it was not physically possible.

Nonetheless, whatever business you are in, it is bad practice to allow your chief rival to have a clear run at a main prize without even mounting a challenge.

▲

Picking up the story where I left it in the Prologue: Mike and I had reached the South Pole after a murderous trek, and had to confront the prospect of carrying on. My own thoughts on the matter were very straightforward, while Mike's motivation was perhaps surprising.

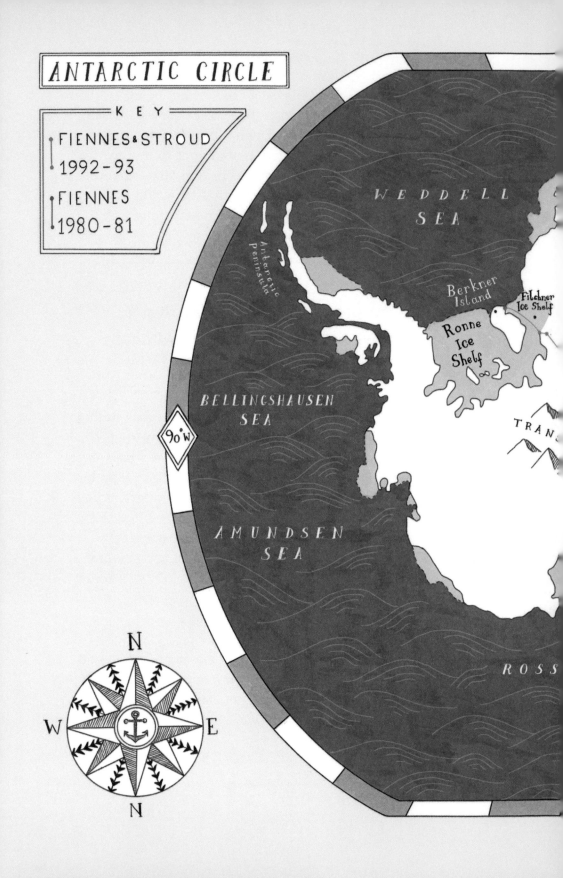

ANTARCTIC CIRCLE

KEY

FIENNES & STROUD
1992–93

FIENNES
1980–81

Antarctic Peninsula

WEDDELL SEA

Berkner Island

Filchner Ice Shelf

Ronne Ice Shelf

BELLINGSHAUSEN SEA

90°W

TRANS

AMUNDSEN SEA

ROSS

N

W   E

N

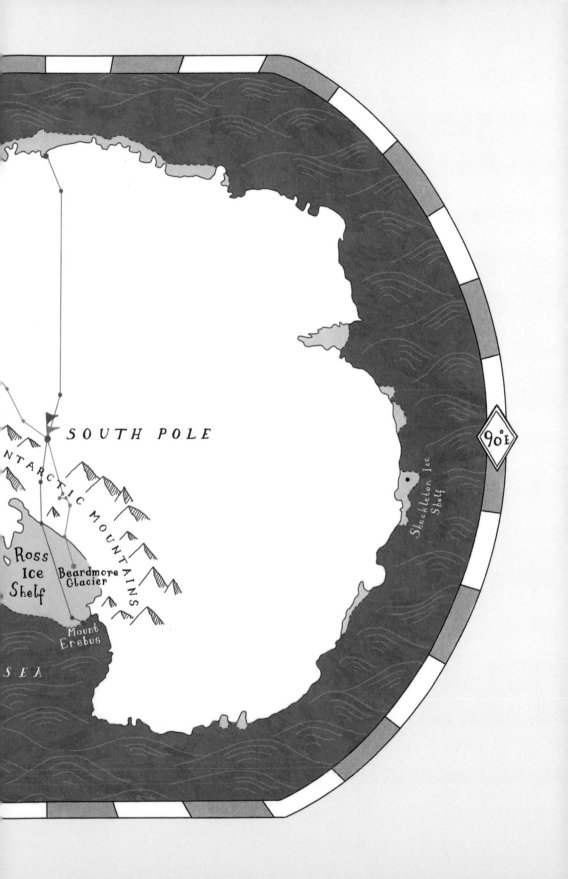

SOUTH POLE

ANTARCTIC MOUNTAINS

Ross
Ice
Shelf

Beardmore
Glacier

Mount
Erebus

SEA

Shackleton Ice
Shelf

90°E

Given his keen interest in the nutritional and physiological effects of our journey and a learned article he planned to write for the *Lancet* on the science of starvation, when we got to the Pole we weighed ourselves. Mike came out of the tent excited by the results. We were starving even more than he had hoped! Keen to find out what would happen to the human body next if we kept going, he was quite determined to do his *Lancet* article even if it turned out to be posthumous.

That sealed it. After spending an hour in our tent at the Pole, we pushed on.

We all have our methods to drive out the mental demons that creep in under conditions of such stress. Mike's term for getting lost in his thoughts was 'mind travelling', a vital form of defence against negative thoughts. The explorer Apsley Cherry-Garrard, on nightmarish Antarctic treks a century ago, repeated endless mantras to himself such as 'Stick it out . . . Stick it out . . . Stick it out'. A favourite of mine was: '*Always* a little further, Pilgrim, I will go.' Any apt doggerel will do and helps to stave off thoughts of continuing pain or the vast distance ahead, on the principle of self-hypnosis.

We all have our methods to drive out the mental demons.

Sometimes I would check my watch and find to my disgust that an excellent run of absorbing thoughts had after all only eliminated a few minutes of reality. At other times, to my delight, I would hear a shout from Mike that I should stop, having exceeded my hour up-front whilst lost in some successful daydream. All day my only guides to reality were my watch and, if it was visible, the sun.

▲

Above: With top
Norwegian traveller
Erling Kagge, 1992/3.

Right: Distractions
included a spot of
chess using urine
sample vials.

Mike Stroud pushes on, somewhere in Antarctica.

Our sledges and equipment began to break up. We lost ski-sticks and spent days man-hauling with only one and, later, with no sticks at all. At length we reached the crevasses above the 9,000-foot descent of the Beardmore Glacier. The daily wind chill was averaging minus 90°. Mike again became hypothermic. His fingers, all bloody and raw, looked revolting.

I preferred to risk Mike's displeasure to any relaxing of my principles of expedition leadership. I like to take democratic decision-making to the brink, but no further. Mike was very understanding, but I knew that he would rightly complain the instant he felt my navigation was taking us into avoidable hazards.

The great mountaineer Reinhold Messner, despite his unrivalled experience in glacier ice-falls, had soon become hopelessly lost on the Beardmore. We had no crampons for the descent of this complex ice-route, but Mike managed to use home-made rope crampons to some effect. This was just as well since he had a twisted ankle which was swollen and painful.

Of the upper stretches of the Beardmore, Shackleton wrote: 'Without crampons each step was an essay in uncertainty where many times a slip meant certain death.'

I knew the rules of route selection for such places. Go for it. Never waste a moment. Pause for nothing and trust your own eye for the best path. So long as the weather and visibility held, we must stop for nothing.

At the mouth of the Keltie Glacier I cheated death when I fell into a narrow crevasse unharnessed and without skis. Only my ski-stick jamming between the crevasse walls jerked my falling body to a halt. Dangling from one arm in the dark void, panic gave me the strength to lunge upwards and escape.

Close by the place where Scott buried his comrade Edgar Evans, frostbitten and hypothermic, we camped under Mount

▲

Go for it. Never waste a moment.
Pause for nothing and trust your
own eye for the best path.

——————

Kyffin. Next day, our ninetieth, we struggled up the ramp of the Gateway and that night Mike wrote, 'We have achieved something very special.' We had walked over the highest, coldest, most inhospitable continent on Earth, from Atlantic to Pacific, with only the supplies that we carried. Somebody might one day complete the journey faster than we had but, like Hillary and Tenzing on Everest, we would always retain the rights to priority.

The Guinness Book of Records stated: 'The longest totally self-supporting polar sledge journey ever made and the first totally unsupported crossing of the Antarctic land mass were achieved by R. Fiennes and M. Stroud. They covered a distance of 1,350 miles.'

▲

The media in Britain reacted to our Antarctic journey in a mostly positive vein, although several letters bounced back this time, including one from John Hunt, the leader of the first ascent of Mount Everest, who reprimanded the *Independent*'s Margaret Maxwell: 'It ill becomes Ms Maxwell to question the motives underlying this astonishing feat of human endurance and courage . . . Surely at a time when, as never before, we need to develop these qualities in the young generation, this story should be accepted at its face value, as a shining example to Britain's youth.'

Also, Dr Geoffrey Hattersley-Smith, a great polar traveller of the 1950s and 1960s, wrote: 'Shackleton's party, without support, covered a distance of 1,215 statute miles. They picked up depots laid by themselves on the outward leg of the same march. It is this record that they have broken. All honour belongs to both Sir Ernest's and Sir Ranulph's parties, men of different eras whose achievements approached the limits of endurance. Comparisons are superfluous, if not impossible to make.'

Another aspect which exercised the media was a supposed falling-out between Mike and myself. It is as if the press cannot believe that two people can survive great dangers together without being at each other's throats with recriminations immediately afterwards.

For eighteen years of polar expeditions Charlie Burton, Oliver Shepard and I managed to survive these post-expedition strains. Ollie and Charlie were loyal and honourable men. They nursed the odd grudge, as did I, but they kept these to themselves and we remained the most solid of friends as a result, and despite constant rumours to the contrary. I can say the same thing for Mike Stroud, my good friend for many decades.

The Director of the Scott Polar Research Institute at the time, Dr John Heap, told me that he considered that Mike and I were 'a marriage made in heaven, with your initiative and drive and Mike's scientific ability'. He added, 'Ran has never sought to justify his expeditions on the basis of questing for knowledge, but he has, nevertheless, contributed greatly to science in the polar regions. He has quietly ensured that good scientific use is made of the knowledge acquired of the areas wherever his expeditions happen to be, by taking advantage of whatever phenomena were before them.'

One tabloid produced a full-page article which claimed to be based on Mike's writings, which began: 'The smiles and mutual backslapping that marked the return of Fiennes and Stroud from their record-breaking Antarctic expedition was a sham and their ninety-five-day trek was peppered with bitter arguments.'

Mike phoned me the day that the article appeared, apologised profusely and explained that he was furious with the newspaper, which had completely misquoted him. He wrote back to the paper to say that they had published 'unadulterated rubbish' and that he hoped to be able to go on another expedition with me before too long. For my part I had no intention of switching from Mike, should another expedition plan crop up.

▲

In the wake of my heart attack in 2003, by far the sanest course of action would have been to retire to the farm and lick my wounds. But I could not shake the idea that Mike had put in my head of running seven marathons in seven continents, in seven days.

When it came to confessing my future marathon intentions, I had hopes that my surgeon Professor Angelini would be sympathetic. After all, he still held the Italian 800 metres record. However, I decided to approach the topic cautiously. Here is his account of his response:

'I saw RF in my office for the usual post-operative check-up and he told me it was his intention to run a marathon. He asked my opinion and I said, as much as I liked running myself, I have never had a patient who had asked me a question like "Can I run a marathon after a heart operation?" I told him he probably could, given the fact that his coronaries were now pretty well sorted out. However I would advise him not to run in a competitive fashion. What he failed to tell me was that his intention was to run seven marathons in seven days on seven continents. Something which I would strongly advise him not to do!'

However, Dr Tim Cripps, the cardiologist, decided that his colleague Dr David Smith in Exeter would be best qualified to decide whether or not I should be allowed to try to run a marathon, since he knew a lot more about sports cardiology.

David, who was a frequent running partner and a good friend to both Mike Stroud and myself and had been my team leader on a race in Morocco, checked my post-operative angiograms with care, and said it would be OK to run non-competitively provided I keep my heart rate low. The bottom line, I decided, was to give it a go and if I couldn't do it then Mike would have to go solo.

So I started to walk, very slowly, on mostly flat ground, and whenever I became breathless or felt giddy, I lay down on the ground until I felt better. Sometimes, if I tripped on uneven ground, my chest hurt where the ribcage had been slit open and it felt as though the wire ties had torn.

I took a mobile phone on each outing and kept calling or being called by Ginny. After a while she agreed that I was approaching things in a slower, more controlled manner than she had thought possible and she did not seem worried by the marathon plan which, unlike most previous projects with Mike, would only last a week. Our charity, which we chose ourselves this time, was the British Heart Foundation, who support the placement of out-of-hospital defibrillators, like the one that saved me. Mike also decided, with Ginny's enthusiastic approval, to take one with us on each run.

My recovery programme was also carefully planned with Ginny's approval:

3 weeks after op: walk for 5 minutes with stops,
    lie down when giddy

8 weeks after op: walk for 30 minutes, no stops

12 weeks after op: jog for 60 minutes, no stops

13 weeks after op: jog for 120 minutes, no stops

15 weeks after op: jog gentle (7-hour) marathon

16 weeks after op: start the 7 × 7 × 7

Dr Mike Stroud, whose warm smile belies a fierce competitive
spirit and a mean streak with injection needles.

A total of 294 kilometres in seven days, the seven marathons would not be at fast race pace, but they would not be gentle runs either. We would need to complete each within six hours, including airport customs and security (in and out). Since none of the scheduled jumbo flights could be expected to delay take-off by even one minute if we were late, I tried to foresee potential airport security problems by writing to airlines in advance, warning them of Mike's metal detector-alarming medical hand baggage and the defibrillator.

The advice from Mike's orthopaedic and sports medicine colleagues was gloomy.

Only eight weeks before departure Mike called me. Bad news. He had been doing a run near his home in Hampshire when his left hip began to complain. He was forced to call his wife, Thea, and ask her to collect him by car to take him home. In a few hours a grapefruit-sized swelling appeared which became a massive blue-black bruise tracking down his thigh. He had an ultrasound check which showed that a small muscle running from the hip to beyond the knee had torn through, and the ripped ends were swimming in a pool of blood. The advice from Mike's orthopaedic and sports medicine colleagues was gloomy: he would not be running anywhere for several months, let alone doing a marathon.

Mike said he was not sure that he agreed with their negative prognosis and would hope to get training again after a short rest. In fact, he took only twelve days' rest, lots of aspirins, some physio and then a test half-hour outing. His hip was sore, he self-diagnosed, but workable.

Our sponsor, Land Rover, decided not to announce the event at all unless we could prove we were fit to run at least two full marathons before departure. Mike chose the Cardiff event a fortnight before our start date and a small marathon near Winchester a week later. Land Rover stressed that we must tell nobody at all about the project until after both trial runs were successfully completed. So I was extremely worried when the Cardiff organisers sent me my running number to stick on my vest a week before their event. The number was 777! They had obviously found out about our main plan. I called Mike, but he assured me that he had not told anyone, and it transpired that the number had been chosen entirely at random. We took this as a good omen.

The Cardiff course turned out to be flat, and Mike, who set the pace, went fast by my standards, finishing in around four hours. I felt drained at the end, but Mike wrote: 'In contrast to me, Ran looked pretty fresh at the end . . . despite the ten years' age difference and his enforced slow training schedule. It was easy to see that he was by far the more natural athlete. But he too had a problem. For many years his back had been the source of much discomfort, causing considerable grief when he was pulling heavy sledges during some of our polar trips. Sadly, running also made it worse and if one marathon exacerbated the pain, how would it react to the hammering it was going to receive? We were both aware that, determined or not, enough pain could defeat us. I made a mental note to add more painkillers to the medical kit.'

The next marathon, seven days later, took us from Winchester to Salisbury, and Mike slowed the pace slightly. We finished in 4 hours, 22 minutes. I had taken ibuprofen tablets and aspirins and felt better than in Cardiff. The Big Seven, we agreed, was at least worth having a go at. We left Heathrow on schedule on 21 October, heading for South America. Land Rover had announced the overall plan of the Challenge the day we left Britain with a simplified summary:

'The team will run their first marathon in Antarctica and the 7-day clock will tick from the moment they start. A twin-engine plane will immediately fly them back to Santiago to run the South American marathon (Number 2). From there to Sydney, Singapore, London, Cairo and finally New York. But they will lose a whole day when they cross the international date line and will have to make this up by running two marathons within one 24-hour period, a morning run in London and another that night in Cairo. If they succeed, the two runners will complete the seven runs in less than 7 × 24 hours and will see only six whole days in terms of sunrises and sunsets.'

Last-minute bad weather caused us to switch our South American leg to Punta Arenas rather than Santiago as originally planned. This just worked out OK due to our meticulously prepared Plan B of alternative flights and venues.

That afternoon we all drove out of town to a long pebble-strewn beach beside the Magellan Strait. At 6 p.m. a whistle from a member of our Chilean support team served as our starting gun and off we loped along the coast before, ten miles later, we turned inland and crossed barren moorland where we flushed out startled groups of rhea, who galloped off very much faster than we could. I managed to stay close behind Mike's shoulder all the way, and our first marathon clocked in at 3 hours, 45 minutes. Back in Punta Arenas we were greeted with the news that a twin-engine jet was on hand to take us, fully sponsored, to the Falklands.

The question has been asked as to whether the Falklands are genuinely part of the Antarctic continent or not. Well, they aren't part of South America and the *Antarctic Dictionary* assures me that Antarctica comprises the continent and its surrounding seas and islands. Support came from quite another direction with the illustrious nineteenth-century botanist, Sir Joseph Hooker, writing about the flora of the Falklands and South Shetlands in his *Flora Antarctica*. It was good enough for me.

'Look left, Ran.' Mike woke me from sleep on our executive jet and pointed out of one of the portholes. An RAF Jaguar fighter plane cruised a few yards from our starboard wing: the pilot's thumbs-up was clearly visible. We landed at Mount Pleasant Military Base. A giant map of the Falklands hung in the airbase commander's office, and we agreed to follow a marathon route he and other officers suggested that led from close to the base to the cathedral in the islands' capital, Port Stanley. We set out with six hours to go before our jet would have to leave in order to connect with the next key flight. We had, therefore, to run this one in under five hours.

At first we were both painfully stiff. Army vehicles passed by every now and again, the drivers hooting and waving. Our progress was being reported on Falklands Radio. There were long climbs and the pebbly road was uneven. We passed by skull-and-crossbones signs, warning of twenty-one-year-old minefields beside the track. In dry areas dwarf shrubs known as diddle-dee spread like heather with red berries mixed with an overall dun-coloured grass, white plumed flower heads and patches of low pig vine. Occasional rook-like birds plunged and soared over the moors. After three hours we passed below Mount Tumbledown, a site of fierce fighting during the 1982 conflict, where British paratroops assaulted Argentinian infantry dug into its upper slopes. My legs began to demand remission. On the uphills as we climbed hundreds of feet, they begged me to stop. I had reached 'the wall' and the time for gritted teeth . . . Fatigue was not my only concern. As Port Stanley grew closer, I kept getting twinges of cramp. These occurred every time we climbed a hill, and this could be serious. You can choose not to listen when muscles cry 'Enough!' which is just a matter of exhaustion, but the body does have other means of making you stop. Cramp in both legs can't be ignored: it simply takes you down . . . My legs were lead when we crossed the finish line after four and a half hours, to be met by Stanley's children, half of the adult population and the Governor of the Islands.

The Governor had laid on tea and sandwiches for us at Government House, but there was, unfortunately, no time to observe the diplomatic civilities as an Army Land Rover rushed us back to Mount Pleasant and hasty goodbyes to the commandant. We made it to Santiago Airport in the nick of time to catch the scheduled BA fight to Sydney with two marathons under our belt and not yet down and out, just tired and aching all over. Before we left Chile we had pared our luggage down to a single item of hand baggage. As the schedule became tighter, we would have no time to wait for baggage carousels at airports.

We reached Sydney on the morning of 29 October and raced through the airport formalities to face a barrage of questions from a curious but sympathetic media, Australians being keen on any form of sporting activity. Then we changed speedily into our running gear. Land Rover Australia had thoughtfully arranged for members of the Sydney Striders running club to run with us in a pack, which was a big help. They included the Australian Iron Man champion who made sure that we did not get lost. The route began near the Opera House, transited the Botanic Gardens, and climbed up and then down the impressive Harbour Bridge, a near nine-mile course that we were to repeat three times, thus ascending and descending the bridge's 104 steps six times.

Mike was feeling much worse. It had started for him in the previous race but now his legs were becoming tighter and stiffer in a way he could not at first understand, and the

Smiles before the reality of our situation really hit home.

competitive edge which we used to spur each other on had not kicked in for him this time. The first signs that Mike's problems were not just fatigue appeared before we left Sydney. His urine was mixed with blood and he suffered persistent diarrhoea. This in turn led to the likelihood of dehydration. But when he weighed himself, anticipating severe weight loss, he was shocked to find that he weighed six kilos more than in Patagonia three days earlier. This explained to him that the tightness in his legs was because of the build-up of fluid in his muscles caused by damage to the muscle cell membranes due to extreme mechanical overwork. What was going on in Mike's body was the result of the abuse to which he was subjecting it, the actual breaking down of his muscles. Not a happy state of affairs given the fact that he had only run three out of the seven marathons and the worst part of the schedule lay immediately ahead. The hottest, most humid run would be in Singapore. And then two marathons within twenty-four hours and ever-increasing jet lag.

We arrived half-asleep and confused at Singapore Airport, and were whisked by our hosts, the Singapore Heart Foundation, to a hotel for one hour's sleep before the press conference they had fixed for 4 a.m. We awoke like zombies, stiff as boards all over. I really did not feel like getting up or walking to the bathroom, never mind trying to run somewhere. Failure, I now perceived, was eminently likely. However, a cold shower, a cup of black coffee and a well-attended press conference, at which we were reminded that we represented the UK, made me realise that withdrawal from the nightmare, at least at this stage, was not an option.

So, to the hooting of horns and the cheering of the sixty Singapore runners who were to accompany us, we set out at dawn to thread our tortured way for the next six hours through the parks and skyscrapers of Singapore. The sun rose all too quickly, as did the roar of the rush-hour traffic.

Singapore was a marathon too far for poor Mike. He was peeing blood and was reduced to walking the last third on jellied legs. His diary recorded:

'Within an hour of starting the Singapore run I realised that this was the marathon too far. I felt sick and my legs, although still painless, had become utterly useless as the first few miles flew by. The heat was stupefying . . . We had managed little more than a quarter of the course before I drew up beside Ran and told him of my predicament. However much I wanted to go on, it was not within my capability and I explained that for me there was no choice but to give in. I urged him to go on running every step if he possibly could. Feeling pretty dismal, I cut back and watched as he and most of our accompanying runners drew slowly away.'

I tried to think of anything that could even briefly take my mind away from the torture.

My back ached. My neck was shot through with sharp pain from the weight of my hung head. I drank copiously from my camelback container of Science-in-Sport drink. I fought against the ever-increasing desire to stop running. I counted my steps. One to a hundred. One to a hundred. Again and again and again. I tried to think of home and Ginny, of the Dhofar war, of Charlie Burton, Ollie Shepard and Anton Bowring on the bridge of the *Benjamin Bowring* in a South Atlantic storm. Of anything that could even briefly take my mind away from the torture of Singapore that morning.

Mike's diary reads:

'Towards the end of our run, the course made a short loop of about three miles with outward and backward paths along the same sector of road. Struggling along, I suddenly realised that Ran was coming the other way. He crossed over and as we approached one another we both raised our hands, which met in passing as the briefest of high-fives. It was a privilege to witness this supreme performance by a man ten years my senior, a man whom so many had recently written off.

'Ran went on to finish, having run every single step, although he still took five hours and twenty-four minutes. I ended up running about two-thirds of the course and walking the remainder, coming in more than half an hour behind him at just over six hours. I was disappointed, but at least I had done the job.'

When the end finally came, I simply fell over under the FINISH banner. The time was over five hours, but the time was immaterial. Paramedics supported me to an ambulance, shoved needles into me and gave me various drinks. A BBC Singapore man with a tape recorder came in and sat on the ambulance bunk. 'Are you giving up?' he asked. He looked blurred to me. 'Yes,' I whispered. 'It would be stupid for me to carry on. But Mike will keep going. I know he will. If one of us can do it, that will be enough.'

Mike said that that run was the hardest thing he had ever done. 'I felt like shit from the word go. The prospect of doing this again in London tomorrow is really appalling.'

Three hours later, and just before our next intercontinental British Airways flight, we were feted at a Singapore Heart Foundation dinner. A doctor gave Mike the report on our body checks, done at the end of the run. Mike believed that we were suffering from something called rhabdomyolysis, which simple tests would confirm by measuring the level of creatine kinase (CK) in our blood. CK plays an important role in fuelling muscle function. The Singapore report showed that my CK level was fifty times above the norm. I was suffering from significant muscle damage. My disappointment in learning this was soon overshadowed by Mike's exclamation as he studied the report. His own CK level was nigh on 500 times the norm, surpassing by far anything he had feared and indicating massive muscle loss. Mike was still up and running through sheer mental willpower alone. His reaction to the news was typical:

'Boarding the plane from Singapore I seriously considered giving up. If things got much worse, I would be in real danger. The blood test results offered me a get-out, a chance to listen to my body's injuries with little loss of face. But I knew inside that there was another way. The risks were manageable if I had further tests with each subsequent race. Giving up is fine if you really have no choice. But if I stopped when I could have done better, I would regret it for the rest of my life.'

We flew on to our next continent, Europe, where London, or rather Heathrow's immediate surroundings, had been the only choice for our fifth run if we were to fit Africa and North America into our remaining forty-eight hours.

On the European leg our race leader was Hugh Jones, one of the best marathon-runners Britain has ever produced and a previous London Marathon winner. He had researched for us the exact route of the original 1908 London Olympics marathon, which began at Windsor Castle and ended at the White City Stadium. We set out from the castle gates at 7.30 a.m. My thoughts as my back, hips, neck and legs creaked into action were centred around the ghastly proposition that, if we managed to complete this run, we would need to begin our next marathon in Africa that same night.

The *Independent* newspaper was clearly wary of our challenge. They quoted a Loughborough University sports science

---

Setting off in Cairo on the second marathon in one day.

professor: 'RF and MS are risking permanent damage and even death by trying to complete their challenge. They could suffer potentially fatal kidney failure because their bodies will have no time to recover between each of their 26-mile runs. They are really punishing their bodies, possibly even to the point of death. We could never get approval from an ethics committee to conduct an experiment on people like this.'

Friends and relations from all over the UK greeted our arrival at White City before Land Rovers rushed us to Heathrow for our flight to Cairo.

The wife of President Mubarak of Egypt was hosting our African run and using it to raise funds for one of her charities, Women for Peace. She had organised a press conference at Giza immediately below the floodlit Pyramids, so I answered the press queries in Omani-accented Arabic, which is perfectly understood in Egypt. We set out at midnight, passing the Sphinx and running alongside some sixty local runners through clamorous crowds of residents busy feasting after their Ramadan daytime fasting. There was an atmosphere everywhere of carnival and chaos, but we ran behind a hooting phalanx of police vans and two ambulances. 'One each,' Mike shouted at me.

We had just run two complete marathons in a single day, and by the time we finished in Cairo, chased the sun three-quarters of the way around the globe, creating about eighteen hours of jet lag.

We arrived at JFK Airport, New York, on time on 2 November and, with the help of a British Airways special assistant, passed rapidly through immigration and customs. Steven Seaton had organised things with great efficiency and we joined some 35,000 other runners for the start of the New York Marathon, a far cry from our first run six and a half long, long days ago in South Antarctica. There, the only other runners in sight had been the odd group of rhea and two penguins.

Steven Seaton and a runner friend of his would, if necessary, physically push us for the twenty-six miles through the streets of the Bronx, the concrete canyons of Manhattan, and finally the green acres of Central Park. The excitement of the great human pack surging forward to the boom of a cannon at the start momentarily made us both forget our delicate states of health, but not for long.

I remembered many, many days on the ice at both ends of the world and over many years when he had been in dire straits and yet kept going.

I knew that Mike was suffering mental torture to keep going in his physical state, but I remembered many, many days on the ice at both ends of the world and over many years when he had been in dire straits and yet kept going. I felt certain that he would make this last run within the rapidly dwindling time reservoir of our seven-day limit, and I was determined that this time we should cross the final line together. So I started running back to find him, which other runners must have thought quite mad.

'Ran was still forging ahead,' Mike wrote, 'but he soon hit on a generous (if painful for him) solution. Unlike previously, he had determined that we should cross the line together. Every few hundred yards he would turn round and drift slowly back to me. Other participants, spotting this figure moving in the wrong direction, must have questioned his sanity. Had they known that this was now his seventh marathon in seven days, he might have been committed. Even with intermittent walking, I began to wonder if I could finish. My legs at times were literally buckling beneath me and this led to an intermittent sudden stagger. Worse, when I did so, I could not help but yelp with pain.'

Mike continued: 'Central Park was a scene of wonder. Each side of the road was lined with tens of thousands of well-wishers and although we had ended up going slowly, there were still thousands of other runners around us. For me, its gentle hills were still utmost tests of resolution, but now there was a difference. From the moment I entered the park gates, I knew for sure that it was all over. Even if I had to crawl, I would cover those final two miles in the two hours that were still left before the clock hit seven full days. I had not done as well as I had wished, for I had not run every single step. But at the outset I did not really think that I would make it at all. Now I was about to complete the undertaking.

'And then there was Ran. He had never stopped running, not even for a single step, in any one of the seven marathons. As I saw him waiting, trotting on the spot, a few hundred yards from the finish, I was so grateful. When we finally crossed that seventh line together, it was a moment to cherish. I cannot thank him enough.'

We finished 28,362nd out of 35,000 runners. The Times editorial the following day said: 'Both men are supposed to be too old to be running so far and so often. Both ignored medical scares and both kept going not by coddling or psychological bonding but by the abrasive competitive spirit that has marked their friendship and rivalry. Their triumph against all odds is not only a magnificent publicity boost for the charities that they are supporting, it is also an inspiration for every runner, every ordinary person, tempted to give up in the face of the impossible.'

CHAPTER TEN

▲

CLIMB YOUR MOUNTAIN

Success is not final, failure is not fatal: it is the
courage to continue that counts.

Winston Churchill

▲

When you see it,
take your chance.

———

I was, in 2009, able to focus on Everest on the 'Third Time Lucky' principle. Marie Curie pointed out that I had become, at sixty-five, an Old Age Pensioner and, if I could summit, I would definitely be the first OAP to do so, which would in their opinion raise over £2 million.

I also had a strong personal motive in summiting as soon as possible, which involved an ongoing race to be the first person to achieve what was generally known in international adventure circles as the Global Reach Challenge.

The first person to describe the summit of Everest as 'The Third Pole' was George Mallory, who died attempting – and maybe succeeding – to reach the summit, and since then the ongoing challenge had been to reach both Poles and to summit Everest. Once that goal was attained by Erling Kagge in the 1990s, the race was on to cross the continent of Antarctica, plus the Arctic Ocean via the Poles, and also summit Everest. I knew that if I could achieve Everest in 2009, I would beat the only two possible contenders for this Global Reach Challenge – Børge Ousland of Norway and Alain Hubert of Belgium.

So I went back to Marie Curie's Thames-side HQ (beside that of MI5) and made a deal. I would try Everest one last time, on condition that they agreed not to allow their highly efficient media department to publicise the attempt until, and if, I was definitely on the summit and not just nearly there.

They found it difficult to accept this condition, since the longer the PR lead time they had, the more donations they would garner from the public. However, they persuaded BBC

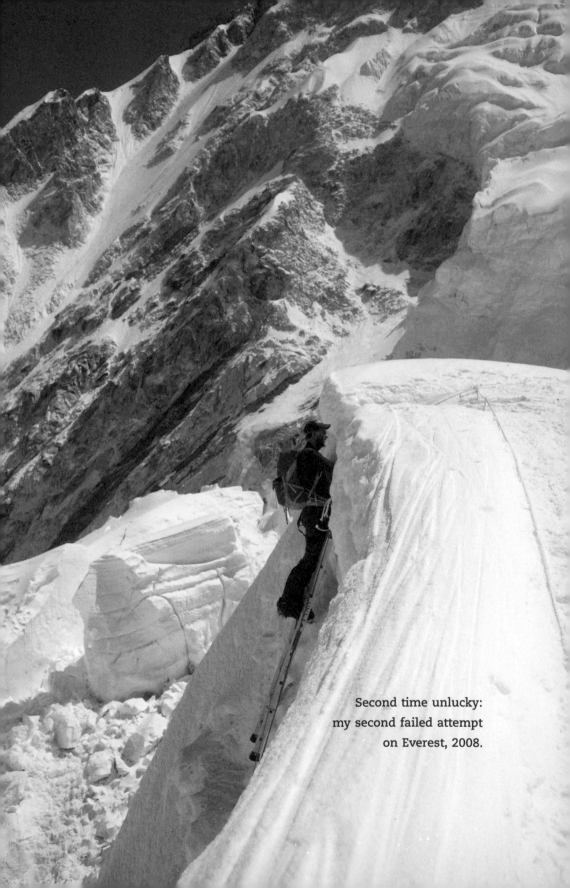

Second time unlucky:
my second failed attempt
on Everest, 2008.

Television News to film the attempt for the national news, which would greatly increase the fundraising potential of the project, and the BBC also agreed that they would keep all their footage off air, *until* I had summited.

Back at the Nepalese Everest Base Camp, the famous Scottish boss of Himalayan Guides in Nepal, Henry Todd, agreed that I could have the ever-patient Tundu as my Sherpa and this time I would go without a European guide, even Kenton, who would be leading another party.

The idea was that, since Tundu climbed with the speed of a mountain goat, there would be no point at all in my making any effort to move faster than a rate with which my body felt happy.

So in late April 2009, I found myself back in the Nepalese base camp, where I trained hard on and above the ledge later ravaged by the 2015 Nepali earthquake which killed a number of Sherpas.

In a separate tent, the BBC News team of producer Mark Giorgio and reporter Andy North filmed our preparations and local excitements such as nearby avalanches. Their cameraman had had to be evacuated by emergency helicopter after falling ill with potentially fatal altitude sickness on the journey up to Base Camp, so Mark and Andy had to teach themselves how to use all the camera and satellite transmission gear brought up on four yaks.

They trained my Sherpa Tundu to use a specific camera for the ascent of and above the notorious Khumbu Icefall. Kenton, leading a small group, set out from the South Col camp on the same night in late May, but a couple of hours after Tundu and I had headed upwards. We passed by the burial sites that this time were covered in snow, and the moonlit slopes were swept only by a soft breeze. Ideal conditions for the steep upper ridges and the Hillary Step.

Keeping to a very slow pace all the way and cosseted by the ever-patient Tundu, I reached the summit, at some 29,029 feet (8,848 metres) above sea level, about an hour or two before dawn.

Tundu shook my hand and, aware that it is stupid to linger in such a place with a limited amount of oxygen and the ever-uncertain weather prospects that had recently killed many climbers, he said. 'Now we go down, Ran, very slowly.'

I reminded him that we *must* first film our reaching of the summit. The team of Mark and Andy had spent over a month producing a great documentary for BBC TV, which simply had to have the 'headline shot' of us on the summit.

Tundu shrugged and unpacked the camera gear. 'Not enough light yet,' he noted.

'We must wait then,' I said. 'Dawn will be soon.'

'Maybe an hour. Very cold. Not too much oxygen. Better we go down. We can film "like" the summit later.'

Knowing how indignant, if not irate, Mark and Andy were likely to be if they were told that we had reached the top but failed to produce any evidence on camera of doing so, I shook my head. I was more fearful of them than any bad consequences of waiting for the light, such as getting cold and running out of oxygen. I thought of our sponsors and of Marie Curie and knew that we could not go down without film, or at least a photo of being on the summit, unless it was a matter of life or death. Tundu shrugged again and, looking resigned, joined me to sit in a huddle on the open space of the summit.

About an hour later and to my intense relief, a well-known Mexican climber arrived and, after greetings, kindly agreed to photograph us. The BBC used that picture in their news headlines and it appeared in newspapers all over the world.

In the icefall with Tundu,
Everest 2009.

With Sherpa Tundu at Summit Everest.

Then, with obvious relief, Tundu led the way down to the Hillary Step. Tundu was a really great person and I was privileged to have been led by him. Sadly he died in an avalanche in 2017.

I was the first ever Old Age Pensioner to have summited Everest.

Marie Curie's fundraising PR made the most of my 'Third Time Lucky' climb, based on the fact that I was the first ever Old Age Pensioner to have summited.

Børge Ousland kindly sent me a card that said simply, 'Well done from Børge.' I never did discover why, as an immensely fit and capable individual, he had turned back in 2004, when only some four hours from the summit.

▲

I turned seventy in 2014, and about that time I noticed some aches and pains, especially in the legs and lower back, which increased at certain times for no rhyme or reason. My old running coach in the Scots Greys, Ernie Newport, had told me his maxim for training older folk. 'Never stop daily exercise. For those who do, that's the beginning of the end.'

The trouble with being post-middle-aged, I found, was that I needed to spend a lot more time trying to keep fit. The most time-effective way of maintaining basic all-round fitness was jogging but, as the years went by, the number of hours needed per week pounding out the miles kept on increasing if I was still to do things that involved fairly strenuous activity. Added to this, I did not really enjoy the training runs as I once had, and was often too busy or travelling when I most needed to put in all those boring jogging hours. My old

---

Hauling a 'sledge' of tyres on Exmoor. Man-hauling muscles
need specific training.

friend Mike Stroud pinpointed my problem: 'Why is exercise so hard to undertake? Boredom, discomfort, fatigue and lack of time must all be contributory, but there is an additional problem. Goals such as good health in old age are far too nebulous to provide the motivation. For that reason, it is often those with a more definite short-term goal that succeed. People who need to lose weight, for example, are more likely to continue to put in time and effort than those who are not too fat. If you give yourself a definite aim, exercise acquires a purpose. You need to set yourself a challenge.'

With Ernie's warning from long ago in mind, in 2015 I decided to enter a race that Mike Stroud knew all about, having done it with a team that he had trained. This was the French Run, the Marathon des Sables.

I approached my long-time sponsor, Harrogate businessman Paul Sykes, and he agreed to fund my training and entry costs. He told the *Guardian*, 'I have sponsored Ran to raise funds for Marie Curie before, including his Everest and Eiger challenges. To date we have raised £6.3 million for them. This has helped many more people living with a terminal illness, as well as providing emotional support for their families.'

The fundraising team at Marie Curie Headquarters estimated that, if I could complete the six-day runs, including a double-marathon, by the official finish time, they would raise some £2.5 million. Due to the heat the race through the sands of the Moroccan Sahara has often been described as 'the toughest foot-race in the world'. You carry what you need in a backpack, including plenty of water.

The week before the race at a Marie Curie-organised press conference, my race-trainer, Rory Coleman, replied to media questions about my chances in the race, 'We've been trying to improve his endurance by running on the Merthyr Mawr sand dunes and on Exmoor. He'll also be training in the heat

Marathon des Sables: day 2.

lab, which recreates the desert climate, in order to test his ability in the heat.'

Rory ran beside me for the entire race, checking the pace, encouraging lots of drinking, and navigating when I lost the trail. On the night-time marathon my head-torch battery dimmed and I failed to spot a pothole. The fall that followed wrenched an area of my lower back, so that for the rest of the race I had to lean over to my left. My race trainer Rory said I had damaged my glutes, and this slowed us down considerably for the remaining two marathon stretches.

The race was being shown on TV in the UK, due to Marie Curie having a film team with a desert vehicle covering our progress at certain points.

Back at home, my wife Louise had noticed my unfortunate post-glutes limp, which definitely gave me a geriatric look. She sent an email to us via the film team that read, 'Elizabeth wants her Daddy back, not a corpse.'

Throughout much of the race, the French organisers had a helicopter overhead (nicknamed *La Vulture*) to remove any runners who appeared to be injured or lost, especially, so the Brit runners said, those with Union Jacks on their backpacks. And, bringing up the rear, were two camels with their severe-looking Tuareg owners, who had instructions to order anyone that they overtook to abandon their attempt.

In a zone of soft sand dunes, Rory looked back and warned me that the 'devil-camels' were only some fifteen minutes behind us. Luckily, they never quite caught up with us and I finished the race as the oldest British runner, and Marie Curie raised a total of £1.8 million as a result, another step to the £20 million we have raised over a lifetime of adventures. I think I could die happy with that on my gravestone.

▲

As I write this, two years off my eightieth birthday and still getting up at 4 a.m. to drive to every far-flung corner of the country to talk about my life, I remain the first person to have crossed both ice-caps and summited Everest (6,000 feet higher than any of the other six continents' highest peaks). Sometime soon, someone, somewhere, will climb all seven summits and go on to reach the moon. I will be watching, and doubtless wishing that it was me.

My advice, for what it is worth, is culled from over half a century of facing up to my quota of life's standard problems, plus a few more self-imposed ones. Funnily enough, I rarely get asked for advice from other adventurers on how to approach a certain type of expedition. What I do get, from the audiences of my lecture tours, is parents asking for advice about their children. My answers are always the same: make sure they get their A-levels; and when they see it, take their chance. I have been lucky in sharing my life, with Ginny and then Louise, with people who helped me to realise my personal ambitions. It's not for me to say that 'luck' will prove the fix for *your* life, but you must watch for it keenly yourself and when you see it, grab it with both hands. That's the best one can do.

I once wrote, before setting out on the epic Transglobe expedition around the world: 'Is it all worthwhile? None of us has made or saved money, followed a profession nor set up any security for the future. We have gained memories and friendships and risked all in the pursuit of an Idea which is still, at the time of writing, a powerful dream to be chased over the polar horizons and beyond.'

Good Luck, go for it, and climb *your* mountain.

Sir Ranulph Fiennes
Exmoor, 2022

First published in Great Britain in 2022 by

QUERCUS

Quercus Editions Ltd
Carmelite House
50 Victoria Embankment
London EC4Y 0DZ
An Hachette UK company

A CIP catalogue record for this book is available
from the British Library

HB ISBN 978 1 52942 633 5

Maps credits: pp. 25, 44–5, 102–3, 204–5 Nicola Howell Hawley

Picture credits: pp. iv-v, 159, 162-3, 168 © Ian Parnell; pp. vi, 227 © Shutterstock; pp. 54–5, 116–17
© Bryn Campbell; pp. 108 © Mike Hoover; p. 112 © Simon Grimes; p. 173 © Kenton Cool;
p. 188 (top) © ALERT; p. 238 © Contreras/BBC; pp. 242–3 © Liz Scarff Fieldcraft.

10 9 8 7 6 5 4 3 2 1

Designed and typeset by EM&EN
Printed and bound in Italy by LEGO S.P.A.

Papers used by Quercus Editions Ltd are from well-managed forests
and other responsible sources.